BLIND SP●TS

What You Don't Know **CAN** Hurt You

"ONE OF THE BEST
LEADERSHIP BOOKS
I'VE EVER READ..."
—Ryan M. Akins
Regional President,
Dale Carnegie

BRIAN BRANDT AND **ASHLEY KUTACH**

This is the most accessible and actionable book written since *How to Win Friends and Influence People*. Brandt and Kutach are authentic in their stories and examples, making them approachable and relatable. One of the best leadership books I've ever read, it focuses on a key aspect of leadership often overlooked—self-evaluation. This book takes the challenging concept of self-evaluation and breaks it into an actionable, simple-to-follow methodology.

Ryan M. Akins
Regional President, Dale Carnegie

Blind Spots brings out one of the great challenges for anyone: to identify and tackle our blind spots. We have used several of these techniques to help our team achieve greater success. As a clinician, I like how it has practical ways to diagnose and then treat blind spots in my personal and professional life. The authors do a great job in delivering practical steps to use personally and with others I manage.

John English, MD
CEO, Bethesda Health Clinic

One of the many strengths of *Blind Spots* is that every chapter is filled with relatable, real-life examples that help you identify the blind spots in both your personal and professional lives. Expect to have many aha moments as you make your way through this instructional, practical, and entertaining read that has the potential to be a game changer in all areas of your life.

Charles Fuhrken, PhD
Lead Editor, Mentoring Minds

The authors beautifully send a clear message on how to continue to grow. *Blind Spots* is full of uplifting examples and stories that lead to powerful changes and inspire improvement on a personal and professional basis. I wish the book had been available when I was a school leader, but no matter your role in life, you will discover practical and insightful direction on developing your potential. A must read!

Sandra Love, EdD
Recipient of the National Distinguished Principal Award and author

Some books take a simple, helpful idea and drown it in platitudes and cute stories. Others actually build something practical around the idea, offering true discovery and transformation to the reader. Personally, I only have time for those books and *Blind Spots* is definitely one of them. More of a powerful tool than a simple book, it offers us a renovation plan for the weaknesses that may be undermining our strengths.

Chris Witt
Executive Pastor of Ministries, Grace Community Church

It is rare to find a book which is practical, inspirational, and pragmatic while grounded in experience and rooted in wisdom. In your hands you have one of these rare instances. It is not just full of knowledge, but the application of situations which sets this book apart and places itself on the hollowed shelf of essential reading. *Blind Spots* is sure to be dog-eared and become the *Velveteen Rabbit* of books because of how often it is referred to, recommended, and utilized throughout the years.

David T. Grout
President, Timberline Team Consulting

Blind Spots is an incredible tool for individuals who want to progress to the next level in any area of their life. It not only provides logical steps to identifying our "blind spots" through the examples and techniques that the authors share throughout the book, but also through summarized action items at the end of each chapter. This will absolutely be on my "read again" list.

Smittee Root
Executive Director, Leadership Tyler

BLIND SP•TS

What You Don't Know
CAN Hurt You

BRIAN BRANDT AND **ASHLEY KUTACH**

To all the lifelong learners who will read this book,
utilize it for their growth, and change the world.

TABLE OF CONTENTS

ABOUT THE AUTHORS

Brian Brandt has spent his life supporting the transformation of individuals and organizations. He is the C.E.O. of Core Insights, a Texas-based company providing premier training, strategic guidance, leadership coaching, and keynotes for businesses, non-profits, and associations. His passion is developing stronger leaders and stronger organizations based on his three decades of leadership experience, including roles such as a C.E.O., public relations director, national sales director, executive pastor, and college tennis coach. He regularly speaks on leadership topics including: blind spots, leadership, effective communication, non-profit issues, and how to bring a vision to fruition. He is regularly interviewed for radio, television, and print media outlets and has written on a wide range of leadership topics. Brian holds a Master of Global Leadership from Fuller Seminary in California, as well as a Bachelor of Accounting from the University of Oklahoma. Brian volunteers for and serves on the board of numerous non-profit agencies. His coaching technique revolves around helping people to discover their blind spots, address them effectively, and move to the next level of leadership.

Ashley Kutach's passion is helping people reach their goals and take control of their careers. She works closely with employees at all levels of organizations to guide, coach, and encourage their development and growth. An accomplished facilitator, executive coach, consultant, keynote speaker, and strategic Human

Resources leader, Ashley provides a perfect balance of compassion and grit in her down-to-earth conversations with others. Her powerful stories, pertinent examples, and on-point suggestions not only spark action but touch the hearts of those with whom she interacts. Ashley holds both a Bachelor of Arts and a Master of Arts in Communication from Texas State University and is a Ph.D. candidate in Human Resource Development at the University of Texas at Tyler. She has spent over 20 years inspiring individuals and businesses to aim high and then take steps to make their goals a reality. She believes that discovering and addressing blind spots is a critical key to success.

Visit **www.CoreInsightsLeadership.com** for more information.

INTRODUCTION

Have you ever experienced a situation where something important didn't turn out as you thought it would, and you don't know why? Have you seen a relationship deteriorate without knowing exactly what happened to cause its demise? Have you missed a promotion you thought you were perfect for—and you're still wondering what went wrong? Were you left out of a project at work without cause—even one where you thought you could really add value? If your answer is "yes" to any of these questions, you've come to the right place for help.

Think of yourself as a new race car. A winning racing team constantly tweaks every aspect of the car in order to achieve greater effectiveness and efficiency. They are never satisfied, always looking for one more modification and one more way to gain an edge over the competition. Now, envision everything you care about most in your life—your relationships, your work, and your community—all working more efficiently and effectively toward a common goal like that racing team. What would it take for that vision to become a reality?

The answer has to do with how much you are paying attention to your blind spots—those weaknesses, problem areas, attitudes, and habits that you're not even aware of that hold you back. While we'll explore the reasons why a blind spot is most often negative, it can also be a positive trait, such as a hidden talent you need to discover. Those who identify their blind spots and commit to working on them are increasingly reaching their potential.

Maybe you're asking yourself, "How can I deal with something I don't realize?" Don't worry. We've been helping people identify and tackle their blind spots—including our own—for years. We'll help you discover time-tested methods for addressing those issues, good or bad, to be certain you're headed down the right path.

In our experience developing and delivering trainings, speaking at conferences, coaching others, and gathering survey data, we've consistently found great benefit in building a framework for clients to identify and deal with their blind spots. What we've learned is so powerful that we felt compelled to write this book so that more people could grow into a cycle of improvement at work as well as in their personal lives.

How to Use This Book

There are three basic steps to follow in order to get the most from this book:

Read—Learning how to improve yourself with greater efficiency is the power that is in these pages, so read with the mindset of application.

Reflect—At the end of each chapter, you will find personal reflection and group discussion questions. Some chapters will also have specific challenges to put what you're learning into action right away.

Learn—You will find even greater value in your reading experience if you engage a learning circle to work through the book with you. Learning circles provide an opportunity for you to gather with a few others for input, insights, feedback, and accountability. A learning circle may involve meeting regularly with an old friend at a coffee shop, a book club, or even a small group of colleagues at the office.

The more you invest working through the discussion questions and challenges, the more benefit you will gain. We encourage you to take time at the end of each chapter to thoughtfully consider each question, take the challenges presented, and if you are reading the book along with a group, engage in group discussion.

CHAPTER 1

Jordan's Story

The better you know yourself, the better your
relationship with the rest of the world.

Toni Collette

Jordan was once the rising star of the organization where he worked. He had fresh and creative ideas, a seemingly endless reservoir of energy, and the charisma to rally his peers and the leadership team. But years later, it seemed as if Jordan's skills were as much a thing of the past as VHS tapes: no longer in demand and obsolete.

How he got to this point in his career came about slowly. One day, for the first time in years, his opinion wasn't solicited on items that weren't part of his direct responsibilities. Then, as the organization engaged in key initiatives, Jordan was somehow left off the meeting invitation list. Over time, he came to realize that his opinion was no longer required because it was no longer valued. Garnering buy-in among his peers, much less those above him in the food chain, seemed to be an exercise in futility.

One morning Jordan remained in bed, not wanting to get up

and go to work. There was a time when he would have sprung out of bed, excited for the day and the countless opportunities that were ahead, but not today. There was a pit in his stomach the size of a bowling ball. He tossed and turned, dreading another eight hours of just going through the motions, averting his eyes as he passed colleagues in the hallway.

He often contemplated how he arrived at this place. Surely, he thought initially, there was a single event that delivered him to this destination. He must have done something seriously wrong. Whenever his mind sifted through his actions, he always came up blank.

This fateful morning, he turned his attention to his boss, Taylor. What if Taylor had poisoned the rest of the team against him? Yes, that was it! His heart began to race as he mapped out the previous few years when his role at the company began to deteriorate. It was Taylor! He began to grin like a detective who just got a break in his case. The sheets and blankets no longer weighed him down, and Jordan jumped up with newfound energy for the day ahead. In his zeal to get dressed hurriedly, he created a clamor that awoke his wife. She promptly gave him "the eye" and rolled over for more slumber. Dressed in perfect style for an era eight years prior, Jordan tossed down a buttered piece of toast with grape jelly and headed to the office.

His problems at work had been like a slow descent on a mountain trolley, and he had only recently started to realize how far down he'd gone. But today, in just a mere 23 minutes before the sun came up, he had pinpointed the issue. It was his boss! Today—today, he told himself, would be the start of his return to his place on the top of the mountain.

And yet his return to the peak never happened.

Why is that?

Jordan's comeback never occurred because while he had

accurately realized the *symptoms* of his demise, he did not recognize the *root* of the problem. The source of the issue wasn't with his boss; it was Jordan.

The following year, new leadership took over the organization. While they recognized the potential Jordan had and the great skills and experience that he possessed, they were also keenly aware of his shortcomings. Specifically, these deficiencies included a failure to stay up with modern practices and technology, a "savior" mentality, and an inability to collaborate. These insufficiencies were diametrically opposed to the type of culture the new regime sought to create. In an effort to help him, Jordan's new supervisor took a direct approach and compassionately shared his perception of the downward spiral of Jordan's reduced influence. He even provided insight into how Jordan had contributed to the problem, but nearly all these observations were met with Jordan's excuses and rationalization.

Jordan left the meeting with his supervisor, fuming with the frustration of a simmering volcano ready to erupt. It wasn't long before Jordan stepped over the line and unleashed a verbal assault on several of his colleagues, resulting in a closed-door conversation and a firm discussion about Jordan's future, or lack thereof, at the organization. Within the week, 18 years of service came down to a going-away party, a less-than-best severance package, a parting gift, and an exit interview.

His sudden firing disrupted Jordan's family and brought a level of stress and strife he had not anticipated. It was months before he found another position, and he took a pay cut that set him back to what he had been making 10 years earlier. Meanwhile, the tension in his home grew more significant. His teen daughters became distressed, as arguments between their parents replaced the amicability they were accustomed to. Likewise, the in-laws became concerned about their grandchildren's stability. Commitments to important charities that Jordan's family had once enjoyed supporting were now delayed, and their plans to save for college were put on hold. The consequences even impacted their social circles, as many relationships were tied to his previous work.

Jordan's former company also suffered when Jordan left, even though their consequences were short-term and outweighed by long-term benefits. The cost of recruiting, retraining, and loss of productivity was estimated at $120,000. Leaders were partially to blame for the loss because they didn't address the issue early enough and help Jordan update his skills, but the culture overall was better off without the person that Jordan had become. Other staff took note from Jordan's situation. They saw that the new management wouldn't accept poor performance, or bad attitudes, and so they rose to the challenge.

Jordan had blind spots. He didn't purposefully head down this path. He didn't seek to put in motion a ripple effect of negative consequences that would impact his whole world. However, his lack of awareness of the potential for trouble, coupled with the unwillingness of others to help him see these deficiencies, did just that. Jordan didn't have a moral failure. He wasn't consciously disengaged. Yet he allowed blinders to develop, and the consequences were serious.

We All Have Blind Spots

Jordan's story reminds us that there are dangers when we allow blind spots to grow and remain in our lives. According to dictionary.com, a blind spot is "an area or subject about which one is uninformed, prejudiced, or unappreciative." It's a form of self-deception and represents an inability to see our own problem. They are in our work environment, and they are very present in our personal lives as well.

Through our coaching, consulting, and training at Core

Insights over many years, we have observed a pattern. Many of the issues that we are asked to address are linked to blind spots. The root cause of the problem is completely foreign to many of the leaders who hire us, and their lack of awareness is significant. Time after time, we've found people—great people and great leaders—who are unable to reach their potential because they've failed to identify and deal with blind spots.

Stories from Others

To get more perspectives on how people experience blind spots, we sent a survey to individuals representing many industries and who work at various levels within organizations with varying work experience. We included three open-ended items in the survey to learn about their experiences with blind spots in the workplace. We asked:

- Tell us about a time that you or someone else in your organization (or previous organization) had a blind spot. What was the blind spot?
- If it was your blind spot shared in the previous answer, how did you become aware of it? If it was someone else's blind spot, how did they become aware of it?
- How did the blind spot impact, or not impact, your/the other person's professional life?

Participants completed the survey online and were able to choose if their responses were to be kept anonymous. We reviewed the responses individually to gather specific stories to share, and then we reviewed all of the responses as a whole to identify potential themes. The results confirmed our suspicions about the prevalence of blind spots and provided rich information that we've woven into the pages of this book for your benefit. While some of the stories and examples shared are from our own experiences, some are directly from the personal experiences provided in the survey data.

Here's one for you to consider—it's a classic definition of a blind spot.

One of the attributes I always appreciated in a previous boss was his ability to quickly make decisions. He was very decisive, and it often seemed as if he had considered every situation prior to them even coming up. He was ready to make a call at any time. I, on the other hand, would contemplate my decision, weighing out the pros and cons. It started out great, but soon we all realized our boss and his strong, quick opinions were the only opinions that mattered to him. He could not see this, and even when we had open conversations, he could never see that he was so strong-willed. Much of our issues were employee-based, so the problem was systemic and affected many. All seemed to recognize the issue but my boss...I talked with my boss frankly, but he could not accept my thoughts. He absolutely could not see himself and his actions clearly. The fallout was employee turnover, yet he was sure it was due to other reasons...I remain friends with this individual, but still hear from other employees that he has not changed.

Everyone has been there at one point or another with someone in authority. Blind spots are everywhere in the workplace. You may not be aware of yours—but there's a good chance someone else is very aware of your shortcomings. They just don't tell you! Consider this observation from a fellow employee regarding the leader of their organization.

The leader was very effective at communicating information but was always frustrated by lack of action of the team. [The leader] thought he was a great "communicator" but he was blind to two-way communication that required listening and gaining feedback. In his perspective, once he shared, others should act.

It was someone else [who] confronted it [after] several years of leading a team and experiencing much turnover with some talented employees. I was not really empowered to use my skills or ability to lead within my area. Better perspectives and ideas within the team were not invited or offered.

One thing that stood out to us as we read story after story like this is that we must want to change *ourselves*. This book is about addressing our own weaknesses and challenges, not changing other people, although that might become a byproduct. Others might be more willing to change, if they see how open we are to improvement. But that's not our focus. The focus is on improving ourselves.

Consider the following story from our survey of someone who wrote openly about her own blind spot and her progress working through it.

When I started my career at my previous organization, one of the first pieces of feedback I received was to work on being more organized. At first, I was surprised and in denial about it. But then when I broke it down and looked at how it was impacting my time management, I realized not only how much of a difference it made but also how easily I could change it. If it had never been pointed out to me, I would have never known the limits it was putting on me to take my job performance to the next level.

My manager gave me the feedback during my introductory performance review. [My lack of organization] stifled the amount of work that I was able to accomplish in a given day. I was bouncing around from thing to thing without practicing follow-through, which led to more work in the end. It made it hard for my coworkers to work around my projects or to assist if I was in the middle of something when I left for the day.

We can't go into a work situation or a relationship with the goal of changing the other person. Remember, the only person you can control or change is you. In the next chapter, we'll break down exactly what a blind spot is—and why it may be holding you back from reaching your full potential in the areas of your life that matter most to you.

○   ○   ○

Personal Reflection

- Has there been a time when you felt like Jordan? If so, what did you learn from the situation?

- Reflect on a time when you saw your organization pay the price for a situation like Jordan's.

- What situations have you observed that are like the other stories shared in this chapter?

- In your own words, describe where Jordan went wrong.

Group Discussion

- When have you seen an organization let a person remain in place, even though they were less effective as time went on? What happened as a result?

- Name some companies, organizations, or industries that were once thriving, but have become extinct or are in deep decline. Why do you think this happened?

- Share a scenario from your present job or a former job where you discovered a hidden talent or skill that you did not know you had. How did you make this discovery? How did the discovery improve your career?

- Share a scenario from your present job or a former job where you missed the mark because of a blind spot in your attitude, relationships, skills, or something else. How did your career suffer because of the blind spot?

- What aspects of the stories in this chapter can you relate to the most and why?

- Is there something that you are being prompted to act upon? Name at least one action step you can take.

CHAPTER 2

What Is a Blind Spot?

The most delightful surprise in life is to
suddenly recognize your own worth.
Maxwell Maltz

When I (Ashley) was learning to drive a car, I remember the day I discovered that even if I looked in the rearview and both side mirrors, there could still be a car lurking nearby that I did not see. As I drove down the highway with my driving instructor, I made a point to carefully and demonstratively check all my mirrors before starting to change lanes. How proud he must be of my efforts, I remember thinking to myself.

"Whoa!" he suddenly gasped, even as I confidently changed lanes. "You didn't check your blind spot." I gripped the steering wheel and stayed in my lane.

I had heard the term before but didn't truly understand what he meant by "blind spot." To prove his point, he asked that I change lanes again, this time checking my blind spot. After once again checking my mirrors, I hesitantly looked over my left shoulder, anticipating moving into the left lane. Sure enough, there was a car just behind me in the left lane, perfectly positioned where it was impossible to see unless I turned my head. Lesson learned!

Looking in the mirrors as we head down the highway of life is not enough. We often hear the phrase "take a look in the mirror" when people suggest studying our own behaviors and actions before making a move. But the mirror only shows us one limited view of ourselves. We likely have undiscovered issues loitering just out of sight.

I recently purchased a car and was impressed by the new safety gizmos and gadgets now available in some vehicles. I was particularly interested in the blind spot detectors installed as a safety measure for drivers. These sensors detect if there is an obstacle or vehicle near the rear of the car and in the adjacent lane. They are so popular that there are even after-market versions of blind spot detectors available for most makes and models.

I can't help but wonder how necessary these devices really are. After all, it only takes a turn or two of your head to check your blind spots. And yet according to the National Highway Traffic Safety Administration, nearly 840,000 blind spot accidents occur each year in the United States, resulting in 300 fatalities! They are a true danger on the road. When driving, it's best not to make lane changes while ignoring blind spots on either side of the vehicle. But we do it all the time—changing lanes without properly looking to see if there is a car just out of view. We might be able to pull it off safely a time or two, but statistically speaking, the dangers of not looking for other vehicles in our blind spots are countless.

Blind spots are not confined to a car. They are also a danger in our personal lives. Simply stated, a blind spot is something that we don't know about ourselves. We don't mean to overlook it—we just don't know it's there. A blind spot can be positive or negative. It can be a bad habit or poor attitude that we overlook. Or it can be a hidden talent or aptitude that we do not know we have, although we're much more likely to be blind to our negative traits.

As far as I know, there is no technology that we can buy to detect personal blind spots. It takes personal effort on our part. We have to look for them and take action.

Johari Window

I (Ashley) first learned about the Johari Window in my freshman year of college during my first and only psychology class. I can remember only two concepts from that class that is now in the distant past: Pavlov's Behavior Modification and the Johari Window. The Johari Window is a technique created by Joseph Luft and Harrington Ingham in 1955 used to help people better understand their relationship with themselves and others. I was fascinated with the idea that I could change the way others behaved by consistently behaving in a certain way myself. In fact, I have used that method throughout the years to assist leaders in achieving their desired results.

The Johari Window intrigued me because of its proposition that that there are things others know about me that I don't know about myself. Up to that point, my eighteen-year-old brain assumed that I knew everything about myself, but I began to consider that this assumption was incorrect.

In the development of the Johari Window, subjects were given a list of 56 adjectives with the instruction to choose five or six that they felt described their own personality. Peers of the individual were then given the same list, and each chose five or six adjectives that they felt best described the person. These adjectives were then mapped onto a grid with four quadrants/windows like the one below.

Johari Window

	Known to Self	Unknown to Self
Known to Others	Open	Blind Spots
Unknown to Others	Hidden	Unknown

Upper left window (Open):

"I know. You know"—The Open window is information that is known to self and known to others. This is the place where communication and trust can flourish.

Upper right window (Blind Spots):

"I don't know. You know"—This window represents our blind spots. This is where self-discovery is a possibility for growth.

Lower left window (Hidden):

"I know. You don't know"—This window is our "mask" and hides things that we know about ourselves and don't share with others.

Lower right window (Unknown):

"I don't know. You don't know"—This Unknown window represents information that we don't know about ourselves and others don't know about us either.

For the purpose of this book, we want to focus on what is in both the Blind Spot and the Unknown quadrants of the matrix. This will allow us to seek insights on a broader range of potential hidden strengths and challenges. Some of our blind spots are known to others; some are hidden to everyone. There is a lot of potential here for self-discovery and improvement.

Your Johari Window

There is a simple activity you can do to utilize the Johari Window to learn more about yourself, the way you perceive yourself, and how that compares to and contrasts with how others perceive you.

First, review the list of adjectives we've put together below and select the five that you feel best describe you.

Able	Idealistic	Religious
Accepting	Independent	Responsive
Adaptable	Ingenious	Searching
Bold	Intelligent	Self-assertive
Brave	Introverted	Self-conscious
Calm	Kind	Sensible
Caring	Knowledgeable	Sentimental
Cheerful	Logical	Serious
Clever	Loving	Shy
Complex	Mature	Silly
Confident	Modest	Spiritual
Dependable	Nervous	Spontaneous
Dignified	Observant	Sympathetic
Energetic	Organized	Tense
Extroverted	Patient	Trustworthy
Friendly	Powerful	Warm
Funny	Proud	Wise
Giving	Quiet	Witty
Happy	Reflective	
Helpful	Relaxed	

Next, provide this same list (without your answers) to five people who know you well. If you want to focus on possible blind spots at work, consider having work colleagues select the five adjectives they feel best describe you. Likewise, if you want to focus on possible blind spots in your personal life, have friends, relatives, or people you volunteer with select the five adjectives they feel best describe you.

Once this is complete, compare your answers to others' responses and place the adjectives in the correct location in the Johari Window.

- Adjectives selected by both the participant and peers are placed in the Open box.
- Adjectives selected by only the participant are placed in the Hidden box.
- Adjectives selected only by peers are placed in the Blind Spot box.
- Adjectives not selected by anybody are placed in Unknown box.

The size of these boxes will likely have to be adjusted to accommodate the number of adjectives in each box. That's okay because the adjustments will give you a good visual of the magnitude of possible blind spots!

Anna's Discovery after Eight Years in the Service Industry

To illustrate what a complete Johari Window looks like and how to interpret the findings, here is a sample from an employee at one of the businesses with whom we work. Anna has worked with this company in the service industry for eight years in a mid-level management role. She completed the Johari Window and also had three coworkers help her by completing the activity.

Johari Window Sample

	Known to Self (words Anna chose for herself)	Unknown to Self (words her colleagues chose but Anna did not)
Known to Others	**Open** Clever Confident Dependable Religious	**Blind Spots** Able Bold Extroverted Organized Powerful Self-assertive Tense
Unknown to Others	**Hidden** Caring	**Unknown** Accepting, Adaptable, Brave, Calm, Cheerful, Complex, Dignified, Energetic, Friendly, Giving, Happy, Helpful, Idealistic, Independent, Ingenious, Intelligent, Introverted, Kind, Knowledgeable, Logical, Loving, Mature, Modest, Nervous, Observant, Patient, Proud, Quiet, Reflective, Relaxed, Responsive, Searching, Self-Conscious, Sensible, Sentimental, Shy, Silly, Spontaneous, Sympathetic, Trustworthy, Warm, Wise, Witty

After Anna completed the Johari Window activity, we visited with her about the discoveries. As you compare the adjectives from the Open section to the Blind Spots section, there is some overlap based on similarity of words. It is clear that Anna has a strong personality and is confident and reliable. As well, it is evident that her faith is important to her and is seen by others. However, there were two aspects that Anna identified as blind spots.

First, she was not aware that she came across as "tense." As we probed and asked follow-up questions, it became evident that the level of intensity with which she carried out some of her responsibilities did not match up with the desired culture of the company she works for. Once this disconnect became apparent, Anna had additional dialogue with her boss and was able to soften some of her interactions with both current and potential clients. The positive results of identifying and acting on her blind spots came swiftly. Because of improved outcomes and subsequent accolades from her employer, Anna was motivated to work even harder to alter her previous behavior with both customers and colleagues.

Anna also discovered a second blind spot, but this one was a positive behavior. She was not aware that her associates considered her organization skills exemplary. Armed with this insight, we encouraged her to proactively utilize this strength in some new ways. When the company began considering a software upgrade to a new system, she volunteered to spearhead the project. By using her newly recognized strength, she demonstrated even more value to the company as she systematically guided a team to assess, acquire, and implement a new methodology and technology solution. Identifying and addressing just two blind spots helped Anna seize some great growth opportunities.

As veterans in the leadership industry, we are more aware of the blind spots holding people back from their peak performance at work and in their personal lives. Unfortunately, the examples we see are way too rampant.

If you're not convinced yet of the enormous threat that blind spots pose to your future, and the equally great potential they have to improve your life once you're aware of them, keep reading. In the next chapter, we'll highlight a few of the most prevalent dangers and lost opportunities due to blind spots.

o   o   o

Personal Reflection

- Focusing on either your personal or work environment (or both), complete a Johari Window for yourself. Next, provide the list of adjectives (without your answers) to five people who know you well. If you want to focus on possible blind spots at work, consider having work colleagues select the five adjectives they feel best describe you. Likewise, if you want to focus on possible blind spots in your personal life, have friends, relatives, or people you volunteer with select the five adjectives they feel best describe you. Once this is complete, compare your answers to others' responses and place the adjectives in the correct location in the Johari Window. Study the results.

- What surprised you during this activity? What blind spots did this exercise reveal?

- How might you utilize this information to better yourself? Be specific with two or three action steps you are willing to take.

Group Discussion

- Think of a close friend or colleague. What weaknesses or challenges have you observed that they seem unaware of?

- When was a time you saw some negative consequences in their lives as a result?

- What strengths have you observed in others that they are not aware of?

- If they became aware of their strengths, how do you think they could capitalize on them?

- Share the results of your Johari Window activity with the group, including any insights you've learned.

- Conduct the Johari Window exercise with your discussion group members. Discuss the benefits of these new discoveries for each member.

CHAPTER 3

How Lost Opportunities Get Lost

Each problem has hidden in it an opportunity so powerful that it literally dwarfs the problem. The greatest success stories were created by people who recognized a problem and turned it into an opportunity.

Joseph Sugarman

I (Ashley) was traveling with two colleagues recently to conduct a training on public speaking. The two of them have known each other for many years and began to reminisce over lunch. "What ever happened to Jason?" one of them asked about a friend they'd known in the past. The other conferred that he hadn't seen Jason in years and last heard that Jason was doing some odd jobs in the town we happened to be visiting. We finished our lunch and returned to the car to drive to the hotel and check in.

As chance would have it, Jason was working the front desk of the hotel! The next day as we discussed the strange coincidence, one of my colleagues mentioned that he would not have guessed 30 years ago that Jason would be working an entry-level job at an age when most people were in the prime of their careers. Evidently,

Jason was a brilliant child and had been an ideal student. He'd held great promise to make his mark on the world, and everyone assumed Jason was destined for success. I didn't know this young man, but I went to bed that night wondering when things changed for Jason. What opportunities did he miss along the way? Why did he miss them, and what insight would have changed the outcome? I fell asleep with the realization that there are "Jasons" in every family, every company, every non-profit, and every community.

Missed Opportunities

We've seen so many examples of people approaching the edge of the career cliff over the years. Tragically, some of them take the plunge and lose their opportunities—all because of a lack of awareness of their blind spots. In your case, maybe a professional relationship soured and you're not sure why that happened. Maybe you did not get that job that was perfect for you. What went wrong? What could you have done differently?

Let's walk through some potential circumstances that might indicate that you have one or more blind spots. Knowing and acting on these areas can make a significant difference and change the trajectory of your future, both professionally and personally.

You may have a blind spot if...

You Are Consistently Not Landing Positions That You're Equipped for

There have been numerous examples where we have seen two candidates vie for an open position at work, with one person losing out simply because of a lack of self-awareness. They don't even realize where they took a wrong turn in the process.

Sometimes it's as simple as not being conscious of what their wardrobe conveys. Many like to believe that what we wear to work should not matter, but research shows that it *does* matter. What we

wear forms others' perceptions of who we are, and those perceptions impact many areas of our lives—including our work.

You may have heard the saying, "Dress for the job you *want* to have, not the job you have." That proverb took on greater meaning to me (Ashley) during an encounter I once had with a new, young female employee. I walked into the kitchen at the office and observed the employee bent over to retrieve a dropped utensil on the floor. Her flowy skirt was short enough to rise up the backs of her legs, revealing her undergarment. I immediately let her know, and she seemed quite embarrassed. I was glad that I had helped so she could avoid such a wardrobe choice in the future. Much to my surprise, I would learn in the following weeks that very short skirts seemed to be a staple of her closet. As the human resource leader at the organization, I decided to re-emphasize with her our dress code policy and how wardrobe impacts us in both negative and positive ways. In our meeting, the employee confirmed that she understood the policy and hoped she "didn't offend" anyone. I assumed the situation was under control. I was wrong. Within the same week, she came to work wearing the same skirt that she was wearing the day of that unfortunate event in the kitchen! She was truly unaware of her blind spot.

For other people, it's something much more significant than their choice of clothing. For example, someone may be well-equipped for a certain position at work, so they wonder why they don't receive the offer they seek. The answer lies in part because they don't have a sense of what their colleagues are *really* thinking or saying about them. They may have all the right credentials and the charm to match, but their self-confidence goes over the line and colleagues interpret it as arrogance. Thus, they're not perceived as a good fit for the job opening, despite having the proper skill set.

As we've conducted countless training programs regarding effective hiring, one of the suggestions we make is for managers to ask questions that will allow them to understand the level of self-awareness of the candidates. For example, we suggest saying: "Tell me about a time when you had a disagreement with someone at work." This is a good prompt to use because it helps to identify what a person cares enough about to convey to others and how forcefully they communicate. Managers can then ask follow-up questions such as, "How did the other person perceive you? How do you know? How was this resolved?" The candidate's answers are important because they help identify their response to challenges, their conflict resolution skills, their ability to articulate complex ideas, and more. Further dialogue can identify if those are patterns or if their example was an isolated situation. In an interview, it's also vital to get a sense of a candidate's emotional intelligence (a concept we'll discuss later), depending upon the level of the position. If the hiring manager sides with the person the candidate disagreed with, this person might not be a good fit. If they came on really strong and adamant, but the situation didn't seem to call for it, you have some new insights into their personality to consider.

You may have a blind spot if...
You Are Rarely Given Special Recognition at Work

Similarly, you may not earn promotions or receive special opportunities to shine at work because your blind spots continue to be unaddressed. When there are unaddressed weaknesses, missed opportunities become the norm, not the exception. At work, this often manifests in being left out of key projects, not being seriously considered for an open position, or worse, an overall marginalization that ultimately results in a lack of high productivity in one's existing position. Too often this is the beginning of the end—a fact that, like the blind spot itself, isn't recognized until it's too late.

While we'll devote later chapters to how to uncover blind spots, it's worth noting early on that there are often cues, clues,

and patterns that we often see only in hindsight. Training ourselves to spot these early instead can both prevent a dump truck of grief over the years and create a mountain of opportunity. The goal is to recognize the issues and reap the benefits as early as possible.

Just this morning an executive in our company came into my (Ashley) office to tell me about a "raving fan" customer she met who uses our educational products and loves the positive impacts the products have had on his school. The executive thought he may be a good customer to use in a formal testimony video for marketing purposes. However, there was a problem, she said. She warned me that his communication skills were not congruent with his education level. Using bad grammar and misusing words was not what anyone would expect from a school principal (one of our target audiences). A video testimony was not going to work. People who are unable to communicate effectively at the level of their education and experience have a blind spot. There's a disconnect. In this example, his school lost an opportunity to be featured as a shining star in our marketing promotion because of a disconnect between what is and what could be. Don't let blind spots rob you of special opportunities!

You may have a blind spot if...
You Have Diminished Health

It's not just our careers and our pocketbooks that suffer the consequences of not recognizing problems. The dangers of not picking up on the signals our body is giving can have serious, and sometimes life-threatening, consequences.

Our office recently started a second round of a popular diet program among employees. At the meetings, employees have the opportunity to weigh themselves. After the first meeting, a colleague shared that she had not weighed herself since she stopped exercising several months earlier. She had been avoiding getting on a scale because then her weight issue would become a reality for her. As disappointed as she was with her weight, she confessed that she was actually relieved to at least know what she was facing.

Sometimes it is too late to change course. More than one person has ignored health-related blind spots, and it led to their death. Harry Houdini was a Hungarian-American illusionist and stunt performer born in 1874. He infamously died of a ruptured appendix when, despite his 104-degree temperature, he refused medical care. Likewise, if we ignore warning signs regarding our health, we may miss a medical disaster headed our way. How much trouble would we save ourselves if we paid attention to early signs of trouble brewing?

You may have a blind spot if...
You Suffer Personal Relationship Troubles

Brenda waltzed into the lunchroom and sat down with her lunchmate colleagues and quickly exclaimed, "Well, here's another chapter to the story." For months, this mother-in-law and soon-to-be grandmother had been sharing her frustration and disappointment with her new daughter-in-law, Olivia. According to Brenda, Olivia never reached out, didn't engage much at family gatherings, and sometimes ignored Brenda's texts and emails.

But now the story had come to a significantly hurtful climax—she didn't get invited to the hospital to be at the birth of the long-awaited grandchild. Brenda shared her strategy was to "keep doing what I'm doing" with the hope that "someday this girl will turn around!" Brenda has a strong personality, and one doesn't have to be around her very long at all before realizing that she's going to say what she's thinking, like it or not.

As she shared the latest news at lunch that day in her typical super-animated way of recounting stories, there was a lot of nodding in agreement. But her colleagues' private thoughts were not quite so supportive, as they considered quietly what it was really like to be Brenda's daughter-in-law.

Then, it happened.

Cindy, who was a lot like Brenda's daughter-in-law and who also coincidentally had a mother-in-law a lot like Brenda, spoke up.

"Brenda, what's your goal?" Cindy asked.

Brenda wasn't sure what Cindy was getting at, but she explained that of course she'd like to have a long-lasting and great relationship with her son, his wife, and their future children.

"Well, I'm a lot like Olivia," Cindy began, "and you're a lot like my mother-in-law. And I can tell you that I don't think you're headed towards that goal."

Brenda stared in disbelief.

It took everything Cindy could muster to go on. "Remember the training from three weeks ago, Brenda?" She remembered the work-sponsored training they'd just completed on personalities in the workplace. Brenda nodded.

"It helped me to understand not only our work environment but also my family dynamics," Cindy explained.

Brenda was completely taken aback and was about to launch into her rebuttal when another coworker named Stephanie, emboldened by Cindy, gently put a hand on Brenda's forearm and calmly interjected, "Just listen for a minute, Brenda."

Cindy proceeded carefully. "Our trainer shared about how each person is wired differently. If I remember right, just 18% of the population is wired like you. So, 82% of the population is not. No wonder your daughter-in-law sounds very different than you! You've got to understand more about what her preferences are and adapt if you *ever* want to move towards your goal of being with your family."

Brenda was now listening intently to what her friend Cindy had to say. "You're very dominating," Cindy explained cautiously, but she was smiling as she said it. "And, you know, you like it," Cindy added. The other coworkers, including Brenda, laughed knowingly and ribbed Brenda.

"Surely, you've seen how some people don't value that," Cindy continued. She then took the chance to refresh their memory about what else they'd learned at the training about how personality differences are tremendously valuable as we take on different roles and responsibilities at work. "If we try to see situations through a different lens, we start to value those differences," Cindy concluded.

At that point, Stephanie jumped in and recalled when the trainer compared interacting with different people at work to international travel and experiencing another culture. "As you all know," Stephanie said, "Bill and I saved up and went to Italy last year. It was a phenomenal experience, but we didn't expect the Italians to adapt to us. We altered our lives to theirs to honor their culture."

Brenda was losing ground and countered, "But Olivia is so reserved! I can't imagine how someone can even function in today's world like that."

Cindy asked quietly, "I wonder if Olivia's all that reserved when *you're* not around?"

Just then, Stephanie pointed to her watch and said it was time for all of them to go back to work. But Brenda kept thinking about this conversation for several days. She went home that weekend and read over her notes from the training. She made a sincere effort to identify where she and her daughter-in-law were similar, although there were many differences. She reflected on how in the world her son could have picked a woman so different than his mother! With a little bit of self-discovery lightening her mood, Brenda started to grin as she remembered what Cindy had said earlier.

"Just 18%...really?" she said aloud, recalling the relatively small percentage of people wired just like her personality.

From the other room, her husband shouted out, "What's that, dear?"

"Oh nothing, just thinking out loud," Brenda said as she reached into the upper left-hand desk drawer and pulled out a note card. "Dear Olivia, " she began. "I'm so glad you're the wife of my son and soon-to-be mother of my grandchild. I appreciate…" Brenda finished the note, put a stamp on it, and felt more at peace about her relationship with Olivia than she had in months.

Thanks to Cindy and Stephanie, Brenda identified a blind spot and started down the path of a mended relationship. Understanding our behavioral style and that of others can shine a spotlight on many areas of our personality that we don't regularly see.

The way we communicate, giving too much focus to work or hobbies, some annoying habits, and not paying enough attention to each other—all these things are just a sampling of the blind spots that develop in personal relationships.

Marriages can share a similar fate. Be mindful of the issues that you have at the start of a marriage and the new ones you develop over time. While statistics vary on the rate of divorce in America, there is little argument that divorce is too prevalent and causes a sea of negative consequences.

Disruptions in relationships affect children, friendships, family, economic status, and much more. It is very likely that you have dealt first-hand with the issues surrounding a breakdown in some kind of relationship. Our friends who are counselors and lawyers tell us (without naming names, mind you) about the growing number of individuals who find themselves on the receiving end of a divorce and claim, "I had no idea my spouse was so unhappy…" Relational blind spots can be devastating. Soon a chasm separates two people who truly care for one another. Remember, a gorge can begin with a small stream. Too often a relational canyon is the result of an unaddressed blind spot that grows over time.

You may have a blind spot if...

Your Working Relationships Suffer

Marriages, friends, and family are not the only relationships that are in danger when we don't deal with our deficiencies. They can taint our working relationships too.

Case in point. Larry and Cedric were the best of friends. Early in 2007, they did a tour together in Afghanistan, serving in the Marines as part of Operation Enduring Freedom. Upon their return to civilian life in the USA, each moved to a different state but they stayed in close contact. Before long, they were vacationing together and their growing families became very close.

Larry developed a notable reputation as an attorney and was asked to serve on the board of directors of a nationwide non-profit where it just so happened that Cedric served as Vice-President of Advancement. Their personal and professional connection grew even stronger.

After an incredibly tense season with his boss and, in Cedric's words, through no fault of his own, Cedric was asked to resign his position. While he was relieved to leave the stressful confines of his supervisor, he had to find a new job to support his family. He assumed that he would get a lot of support from Larry, both emotionally and through Larry's business connections. That's when Larry "went dark" on Cedric. Larry's obligations as a board member put him in a precarious position and he felt awkward communicating with Cedric.

Not only did he not reach out across the miles as Cedric expected, but also Larry didn't respond to communication in a timely way. Cedric, frustrated by Larry's behavior, wrote Larry off as a friend. Years later, they had a cordial but awkward conversation at the funeral of a mutual friend. Many years later, Cedric moved to Larry's city and the two men decided to have lunch one day.

Cedric started out the conversation apologizing for the

assumptions and expectations he had made. He was blind to it before, but he now realized that as a board member, Larry had been in a precarious spot when Cedric was let go. They decided that day to start afresh and put the past behind them. They're not best friends now, but they've at least opened the door and are beginning to bridge the chasm created by the lack of dialogue and attention in their relationship.

Your organization may have a blind spot if...
They Fail to Heed Warnings

Sometimes whole organizations experience blind spots. In 2013 a multi-story garment factory in Bangladesh collapsed, killing more than 1,127 workers and injuring roughly 2,500 more. The building contained a bank, apartments, multiple clothing factories, and other shops. Cracks in the structure had been forming for a while, resulting in some parts of the building being closed off. Warnings that the building was unsafe went ignored, and some workers were threatened with termination if they did not return to work.

What was so clear to some became a tragic consequence for many. The signals were there, but they were ignored.

Structural deterioration doesn't just happen to buildings; it happens to the very essence of companies. For example, one of the worst economic seasons in recent history was the result of some purposeful sub-prime lending tactics. From 2004 to 2006, sub-prime mortgages rose from the historical 8% or lower range to approximately 20%. Those in charge completely ignored the risks and warning signs of this trend, and several major financial institutions collapsed in September 2008 as a result. The consequences of ignoring these warnings included a significant disruption in the flow of credit to businesses and consumers as well as the onset of a severe global recession.

The Dangers of Blind Spots

Whether it's our careers, our relationships, our health, or the organizations where we work, the dangers of neglected blind spots are disconcerting at best and catastrophic at worst. Now that we're fully aware of the damage blind spots can do in many areas of our lives, we'll explore their root causes in the next chapter. There are many reasons why people have blind spots. Some of the most common reasons are tied to things like stereotypes, misinformation, and a general lack of self-awareness. Understanding what has caused your blind spot will not only help you determine how to take action but also assist you in avoiding potential trouble in the future.

o   o   o

Personal Reflection

- Think of someone you know who is not living up to their potential. Why do you think this is happening?

- What successes have you witnessed others achieve in a personal or professional environment that you've missed out on? What did they do differently to achieve that level of success?

- What are the ingredients of a healthy physical life? What habits contribute to or detract from those components?

- What relationship challenges have you experienced in the past at work? Why?

- What key personal relationships have you started but didn't maintain? Was a blind spot the cause? Explain.

- When have you misread a situation at work or in a personal setting? In hindsight, was there something you missed? What would you do differently if you could do it over again?

Group Discussion

- Why do you think that people often make excuses instead of recognizing that a blind spot has caused a missed opportunity?

- When was a time that you experienced a missed opportunity at work or in a relationship? What follow-up action did you take once you realized it?

- What processes, habits, and/or action steps could you put in place to ensure you don't miss other key opportunities at work or in your personal life?

- Talk about a time when you felt very successful and fulfilled. Next, share a time when you did not feel as successful or fulfilled. What else was happening in your life that made you feel that way in both scenarios?

CHAPTER 4

Stereotypes and Labels Holding You Back

It ain't what they call you, it's what you answer to.

W.C. Fields

In my (Brian) backyard, I have numerous pine trees that tower over 70 feet tall. Like many parts of the country, we also have unruly vines growing up the trees as well. About two years ago, I decided to eradicate my trees of these vines because I was concerned that they would eventually cause issues. I cut the vines at the root and proceeded to pull most of them down one by one. I couldn't pull down all of the vines in the top layers of branches, but what I did manage to remove looked so much better!

After returning from a vacation soon after, I walked outside and discovered that in the short amount of time I was gone, four feet of new vines had already started to make their way up my trees! I quickly and effortlessly pulled them away from the trunks. But despite the fact that the remaining clumps of vines high in the branches are no longer being nourished (because I cut them at the root), I still cannot remove them. I let them have their way too long and from my vantage point on the ground, no amount of tugging will get them down. I could hire professionals with the skill and equipment to get high enough to painstakingly loosen the vines from the hold they have on the tree, but I cannot do it on my own.

So it is with some of the issues in our personalities and/or behavior. They are easier to address if we "cut off" the issues at the root and do so early before they become ingrained habits. It takes more energy and effort (and perhaps some professional coaching or counseling) to properly address them if we wait.

The following are some common root causes of blind spots and deficiencies that lead to missed open doors and prime opportunities. We won't present strategies to solve these yet, as they will be discussed later in the book. But we do need a comprehensive understanding of how blind spots, like those vines, are strangling our potential.

Root Cause of a Blind Spot: Stereotypes

Remember—blind spots can also be positive traits that we don't see in ourselves. Stereotypes regarding our race, gender, age, and other "labels" we place on ourselves can greatly limit our opportunities. They cause us to believe certain untruths about ourselves that may blind us to the real abilities and talents we possess. Often these misconceptions begin early in our lives and quickly shape who we become. Some common stereotypes include phrases like, "Men are strong, so they do all the work." Or "Women are not as capable as men." You could probably add more to this list very easily. Because of the delicate nature of stereotypes and the fact that they are not rooted in truth, we are uncomfortable even putting them in writing. However, it's important to gain a clear understanding of them so that we can consider if and how untruths have shaped our lives and the lives of others.

When I (Ashley) was growing up, little girls were encouraged to become teachers or nurses. We often played "school" at recess or took care of our stuffed animals as if they were ill patients. There is an argument that says we played these games because caring and nurturing are natural to girls. In general, that point has been proven true. The problem is that this belief is a generalization. Some girls do not fit that mold, but often spend a lot of time trying to do so. Therefore, they miss out on opportunities to pursue activities better aligned to their talents and interests.

Likewise, many young boys who could have made exceptional teachers or nurses were told that these professions were "for girls." I would argue that many never recognized their potential in a fulfilling career because of the social stereotypes placed on them. Similarly, many girls missed out on a fulfilling career while they trudged along as teachers and nurses, a noble profession, but it was not for them.

Columbia University provost and social psychologist Claude Steele performed research with college students to test the effects of both positive and negative stereotypes and wrote a book on his findings titled *Whistling Vivaldi and Other Clues to How Stereotypes Affect Us*. Steele found that positive stereotypes boost performance (both on academic and athletic tasks), while negative stereotypes hinder performance. One of the reasons this occurs is that when someone believes their population (a specific gender, race, age, etc.) is "good at" a certain task, they will attempt the task more times and endure more frustration before they decide if they are, in fact, good or bad at the task. If a person believes a negative stereotype about their population performing a certain task, they either won't even try or will stop as soon as the task is the least bit challenging. They assume that the stereotype is correct, so they give up.

Steele's research is very compelling. One of the most surprising examples of his research involved administering a math test to a group of male and female students. One group was told that typically females do not score as well as men on the test. The other group was told that females often scored as well as males on this test. What were the results? They reflected self-fulfilling prophecy—a prediction we make about ourselves that we help prove to be true. In the first group, the females did not score as well as the males, but in the second group they scored equally well. Why? Because if a group of people already assumes they will not succeed at something, they will not do their best in most cases.

What might you believe about yourself that isn't true? What career, hobby, pursuit, or interest have you considered trying but stopped because what someone led you to believe about yourself keeps you from trying? We challenge you to identify an aspect of your life where the self-talk from a stereotype is holding you back and fight it.

Every year, our area Chamber of Commerce brings in an economist to speak. For many years, it's been Dr. Ray Perryman, who has a litany of accolades, awards, and accomplishments. The first year that I (Brian) went to the annual meeting, I had really low expectations. I stereotyped economists as boring speakers who didn't know how to connect with their audience. Wow, was I wrong! Ray always has tremendous mastery of the data, but he delivers it in such a way that the common person can comprehend it. He starts at a global level, then moves to the United States level, then to the state level, and ultimately to his audience's home area to help people really understand what is taking place with the economy. He weaves in stories and examples and has an outstanding sense of humor. I'm glad Ray didn't buy into the idea that "economists can't be good speakers." Now, I relish the opportunity to invite people who are new to the area to this annual event and watch their reactions to this rock star economist!

Martin Seligman wrote *Learned Optimism: How to Change Your Mind and Your Life* and introduces readers to the concept of "learned helplessness"—another way stereotypes affect us. He uses a powerful illustration to explain how they can overcome feeding this negative feedback loop. Imagine dividing a home aquarium in half with a see-through panel. Then, fill the aquarium with water. On one side, add some small bait fish. On the other side, add a barracuda. Then watch what happens. The barracuda repeatedly but unsuccessfully tries to attack the bait fish, but eventually the barracuda tires of bumping into the glass panel separating them and quits trying. It assumes that it will only hurt itself if it continues.

Imagine then, Seligman says, that you remove the clear panel separating one side of the tank from the other. What do you think will happen next? Most likely, the barracuda will realize the golden opportunity to now sate his appetite, right? Surprisingly, that's not what happens. It has learned that no matter how much it tries, it cannot get to the bait fish. Furthermore, it has learned that repeated attempts at doing so will hurt. It has developed "learned helplessness" so it doesn't even try. Because of previous failures, the barracuda is now blind to the opportunity before it.

Seligman points out that we often make false assumptions about adversity that make us helpless. These assumptions include permanence, pervasiveness, and personalization.

- **Permanence** expresses how we think about our adversities. If we describe our situations in terms of "always" or "never," we reveal an assumption that our adversity will be permanent. For example, "Problems like this always happen to me" or "It seems like I can never win."
- **Pervasiveness** expresses how widely we assume our adverse circumstances to be true. For example, someone can over-generalize and say, "Women never get ahead." Or they can dial down the pervasiveness to be more specific and say,

"Women are not promoted into executive positions *at this particular organization.*" Both demonstrate two different views of pervasiveness, but one is more paralyzing than the other. Exaggerating the pervasiveness of a problem keeps us from becoming all we can be.

- **Personalization** describes the person or thing that we blame for our negative circumstances. If we primarily blame ourselves, we internalize. If we primarily blame other people or circumstances, we externalize. Blaming others is not a positive workplace behavior, and self-blame is often associated with a low self-esteem. Are these attitudes holding you back from trying to succeed or improve?

Root Cause of a Blind Spot: Misinformed Messages and Labeling by Others

I (Ashley) was the second child in our family, and my older brother loved to talk. He still does. I didn't talk much at all during the first 10 years or so of my life. I'm not sure if that was because I didn't like to talk or because my brother was always talking for both of us! My mother always explained to others that I was "shy." Therefore, I grew up calling myself shy. I still call myself shy. Am I shy? I'm not certain. The people around me (coworkers, friends, family) don't think so. Did I really spend all those years in silence because I was shy? And how has that label shaped my perception of myself?

When parents carelessly label their children, kids often feel as if they can't escape that label. Parents and caregivers label children unintentionally and intentionally at times; sometimes they do so with a sense of fun and humor and sometimes out of anger or frustration. No matter how the labeling is done, it can limit children in the activities they try, therefore limiting their ability to succeed in areas.

Where stereotypes are generalizations (e.g., women are not as athletic as men), messages and labeling are much more specific and they are aimed at you personally. These messages can be correct or incorrect. Much like stereotyping, these messages usually begin to creep into our psyche early in childhood. The labels others put on us in childhood are often labels that we then put on ourselves in adulthood. If you were told by a significant other that you were not athletic, you most likely still feel and say, "I am not athletic."

Labels often placed on people include good and bad examples like these:

- You are not smart
- You are slow
- You are not pretty enough
- You are not good at (math, reading, writing, science, etc.)
- You are not athletic
- You are an artist
- You are beautiful
- You are outgoing
- You are shy
- You are giving
- You are stingy
- You are not college material
- You are too tall/short

Read that list again. Did something resonate with you? Was there something you've heard before or a label that you allowed to be placed on you? You're not alone. It happens a lot, but it doesn't have to be that way.

In the fall of 1978, basketball superstar Michael Jordan was only a sophomore at Laney High School in Wilmington, North Carolina. Standing at only 5 feet 9 inches tall, he was cut from the varsity team. The coach decided to use 6-foot 8-inch sophomore Leroy Smith instead. Michael just wasn't tall enough. By the start of the next season, Michael had grown five inches and became the first player in the school's history to average an impressive triple-double. In basketball, a double occurs when a player obtains a double-digit total in any one of five categories—points, assists, rebounds, steals, or blocked shots—in a single game. A triple-double occurs when a player does that in three of the five categories…quite a feat. He eventually led the team to a state championship. It's a good thing Michael did not let "being too short" stop him. What's stopping you?

Root Cause of a Blind Spot: Lacking Self-Awareness

Another reason people miss opportunities is a lack of self-awareness. How can it be that we have been with ourselves since the day we were born, yet are completely unaware of certain things about ourselves? If you don't believe us, draw a picture of one of your ears and see how accurate you are. It's been there your whole life, but you're probably not familiar with its intricacies. Some people are very self-aware, and others are not self-aware at all.

During a recent lunch date with an acquaintance, we witnessed a customer speaking rudely to the server. My (Ashley) friend turned to me and stated, "I could never be so rude to someone." I stared at her wide-eyed in disbelief. She was often rude to strangers and friends alike. In fact, many of our mutual friends had stopped spending time with her due to her behavior. How could someone be so out of touch with their own actions and personality?

Self-awareness is typically born from taking risks, trying new things, learning from successes and failures, and breaking out of our comfort zone. These opportunities allow people a chance to self-discover. People also learn about themselves by reading other people's reactions to them. When we properly read people, we can adjust what we say or how we behave at the present moment and in future situations.

In our experience, people who are not very self-aware don't do a great job of reading verbal and non-verbal feedback provided by others. I'm sure you've been in a meeting where some people dominated the conversation. Every time a question is asked, they speak over people, or they're the first to speak. It's good for us to recognize when we're not contributing enough or contributing too much. Understanding non-verbal cues can help us observe how people are perceiving us, their reaction to our phrasing, or how much agreement we have on a subject.

Recently, I (Brian) facilitated a strategic planning session at a venue. I had sent a diagram of the desired setup for the room, but when I showed up for the event it wasn't ready. I checked in with the staff and realized there had been a miscommunication on their end. We were able to rectify the situation with a little bit of extra sweat and urgency.

At the end of the day as I was packing up to leave, the owner of the facility approached me. She was very sorry for the mistake and hoped that the oversight didn't have a negative impact on our session. I responded back, "They didn't have a clue!"

For a fraction of a second, she looked uncomfortable. Recognizing that micro-burst clue to what she was thinking, I suspected she had misunderstood (understandably) who the "they" was in that sentence.

I said, "Let me clarify...our *participants* never knew that it wasn't set up."

She smiled, relieved that I wasn't calling her employees "clueless," and we were able to move the conversation along. Imagine the barrier to a strong relationship that might have formed if I hadn't picked up on her non-verbal communication. By reading people properly, we can make real-time adjustments and capture key learnings that change our trajectory.

According to Dr. Travis Bradberry, author of *Emotional*

Intelligence 2.0, "a lack of self-awareness will actually hold you back from developing self-management, social awareness, and relationship management skills." In other words, lack of self-awareness can cause blind spots that will prevent you from experiencing higher levels of success and relationship fulfillment.

One day I (Brian) was reading by the side of the pool when my teenage son asked me, "Have you ever read a book that doesn't have 'leadership' in the title or subtitle?" He was being funny, but he brought up a good point. For the last few years, I had been working on a master's degree in Global Leadership and had conducted a lot of consulting, coaching, training, and speaking that had fueled my desire to read a lot of leadership books. But that day I realized that I was missing out with my limited selections. So, as I set my goals for the coming year, I determined that half of my reading had to be fiction. It wasn't long before I regularly escaped into the Jack Reacher world that Lee Child created!

Many people claim to be self-aware, but the truth is that most people are at least partially blind to their personal attributes, habits, and patterns. Seek to grow in these skills so that you can self-coach to greater success. You can start with something small. One night before dinner, I (Brian) asked my youngest child to set the table. As we started dinner, I noticed she'd neglected to put a knife at my place setting. I jokingly said to her, "So, you didn't think I deserved a knife?"

My oldest daughter commented, "Well, aren't *you* passive-aggressive tonight?"

I just grinned, but her comment made me think a little bit more about my reaction. The phrase "passive-aggressive" seems to be thrown around a considerable amount, and I started wondering if the technical definition matched with the popular preconceived notions. After the table was cleared and the dishes were done, our family started working on homework and I decided to read up on passive-aggressive communication.

It soon struck me that I was indeed being passive-aggressive with my daughter. What's worse, I realized that the dinner table situation wasn't an isolated incident. I could think of far more instances than I desired where I had been passive-aggressive with my wife! For the next week I decided to pay more attention to when and how my passive-aggressive tendencies, actions, or verbiage showed up. While they weren't daily occurrences, there were more than I liked.

After a few days, I pulled my wife aside, confessed, and apologized. She was very gracious and appreciative that I had recognized this weakness and sought to deal with it. Several months later I can tell you that while I may not have eradicated passive-aggressive tendencies from our relationship, they are certainly less frequent. I also later thanked my daughter for bringing it to my attention.

I must not only stay vigilant to watch my behavior but also seek to understand the root cause and address it. I discovered that in light of my behavioral style (a strategy for addressing blind spots that we'll discuss shortly), I tend to get sarcastic when I feel a lack of recognition or esteem is present. By verbalizing my newfound awareness to my family, I heightened my recognition of the problem. And doing so also gave them greater permission to call me out on being passive-aggressive as well as on other issues that I'm facing.

Root Cause of a Blind Spot: Lacking Others' Awareness

I (Ashley) once hired a new employee for one of our teams. As always with a new hire, the team was excited and looked forward to teaching her, learning from her experiences, and sharing the workload. Unfortunately, the new employee didn't integrate into the team as well as we had anticipated. She mostly kept to herself and didn't seem to be working very hard. I had personally noticed lack of eye contact and some quirky communication habits that surprised me, as I had not noticed them during the interview process.

The team quickly grew frustrated. I started meeting with the employee weekly to provide coaching related to her social interaction with others and the lack of tenacity shown in her work. In the first of these coaching sessions, I started by asking how things were going in her new role. She said things were great. She loved the job and was happier than she had ever been at work. Her response threw me because from the team's perspective she clearly wasn't fitting in with the rest of the members. She seemed blissfully unaware of the others' view of her. As I brought up specific examples each week of observations I made, she was surprised over and over again. She really didn't seem to know how we were perceiving her. After about a month of these coaching sessions, I stopped asking her how things were going because those questions were not fruitful. I began to ask more specific questions such as, "Tell me about one challenging task that you completed this week." She would think for a few seconds and say, "Nothing really. Everything was really easy this week." Impossible. We had challenging roles and faced challenges daily, maybe even hourly. I realized that her complete lack of awareness of others' perceptions was going to be a mountain for her to overcome.

Here's another common instance at work. We all know adults who talk on and on without regard for the non-verbal cues they are getting from their weary audience. You may try different tactics to redirect the conversation—interrupting, changing the subject— anything to signal that you're ready to move on to something else. However, this type of person is completely unaware of how others feel, their needs, or their thoughts. Therefore, they exhibit behaviors that drive people away.

Not assimilating well or talking too much are just two examples of a common blind spot that results when we tune out the needs of others. Other examples include overlooking personal hygiene, talking over people, tapping, and voice modulation issues. Most of the time, other people will give the offender feedback—both verbal and non-verbal—but it's often ignored.

Get Ready to Work

In the next chapter, you'll learn specific ways to identify your own blind spots. It will take courage to recognize and deal with your weaknesses—but it will ultimately lead you to reach your peak performance at work, and you'll notice a difference in the quality of your relationships too.

∘   ∘   ∘

Personal Reflection

- What common stereotypes fit your gender, race, or age? Note the ways you defy these stereotypes in your daily life. Which ones do you struggle with?

- What labels—good and/or bad—were placed on you as a child? How do you think they impacted the person you have become?

- Rate the following on a scale of 1 to 10, 1 being "I don't know how well I do this" (the least self-aware) and 10 being "I have an accurate picture of my performance" (the most self-aware):
    a. Your current job performance

    b. Your relationships with others

    c. Your ability to manage your time

    d. Your listening skills

    e. Your self-discipline (diet, exercise, sleep, etc.)

    f. Your ability to communicate your point of view

    g. Your leadership ability

- What evidence do you have to support your answers?

- Consider a time recently when the outcome of a job opportunity or a relationship didn't go as planned. Were there any signals that you missed that it was heading in the wrong direction? How did you react?

- Choose three people who will be honest with you about your personality and behavior. Ask them the General and/or Specific questions from the Personal Feedback Worksheet in Appendix A. What insights did you discover about yourself?

Group Discussion

- How does society perpetuate stereotypes about others?

- Think about someone close to you who has a blind spot. Based on what you learned in this chapter, what do you think may be the root cause?

- If you're comfortable in the group, share a stereotype, label, or misinformation you've believed about yourself and how it is holding you back from reaching your potential.

CHAPTER 5

Pay Attention.
Then Ask Good Questions.

Searching is half the fun. Life is much more manageable when thought of as a scavenger hunt as opposed to a surprise party.

Jimmy Buffett

In the early morning hours of September 15, 2001, just four days after the terrorist attacks, five cars in Texas drove into the dark night and tumbled over 80 feet into the water below. When they entered the 2.37-mile-long Queen Isabella Causeway that connects the mainland of Port Isabel with the popular tourist spot South Padre Island, they had no idea that up ahead at the bridge's peak was a 240-foot gap. A tugboat pushing several loaded barges had veered off course earlier and struck the bridge, causing the support pillars to collapse. The unsuspecting drivers, without any reason for concern, drove right into the gap. Eight people plunged to their deaths.

Let's contrast this sudden tragedy to the tornado that devastated Joplin, Missouri, on May 22, 2011. The F5 tornado struck the city with maximum winds over 200 miles per hour, resulting in more than 160 deaths and 1,000 injuries. This was the first tornado to claim the lives of more than 100 people since the Flint, Michigan, tornado in 1953. The casualty numbers were astounding, given the fact that unlike those drivers on the bridge, residents had advance warning. In fact, the National Weather Service Central Region Service Assessment's report showed that appropriate warning was provided, but most Joplin residents did not respond initially. Others did not react or reacted too slowly to subsequent warnings. Why did so many people not respond?

According to researchers, people ignore weather warning signs for many reasons. Accuweather.com even published an article summarizing why people are not better prepared for disaster when warnings of impending danger are issued, citing the following reasons:[1]

Complacency: We're both guilty of this one! We live in a storm and tornado rich area, and our county often has severe weather and tornado warnings, so we assume that storm warnings are not cause for much concern.

Need for confirmation from multiple sources: Most people want to be told from multiple reliable resources like the Internet, television, etc., before they are willing to take action. Sometimes that causes them to act too slowly.

"It won't happen to me" attitude: People often assume that it "won't happen to me." So, they don't act.

Poor communication of the danger: People may not live within earshot of the emergency warning systems. The more mediums used to warn people, the better chance that the word will get out.

Not taking the right course of action: Many victims take cover in a center room in their house and avoid windows. This may be the right course of action in a solid structure, but it's not the right course of action in a mobile home, for example.

What do these examples have to do with blind spots? Sometimes blind spots have no warning before we see them, but usually there are plenty of signs before they cause damage. We just have to be paying attention.

Some People Ignore Danger

The reasons why people ignore dangerous weather warnings and why people routinely overlook blind spots in their personal and professional lives are remarkably similar. Think about it:

- **Complacency:** Warning signs may come in the form of a friend's advice or an unfavorable personnel review. People sometimes feel that the warning signs are not indicative of something serious. They may think things are "good enough" in their lives, so change isn't necessary.

- **Need for confirmation from multiple sources:** Most people need to be told from multiple reliable resources (family, friends, colleagues, counselor, etc.) that they have a problem before they are willing to take action—and even then, they act too slowly.

- **"It won't happen to me" attitude:** People often assume that whatever may be holding them back from reaching their potential at work or threatening a valuable relationship is not *that* serious. Again, many people claim they never saw a tragedy like a sudden loss of employment or a divorce coming.

- **Poor communication of the danger:** The more books, speakers, articles, confrontations, and affirmations to warn people about blind spots, the better chance there is that they will get the message.

- **Not taking the right course of action:** For example, when someone is told that their choice of words in their weekly staff meeting is offensive, they decide they're just "not going to say anything." A better approach would be to choose their words more carefully and measure how their new approach is being perceived.

I (Brian) have a friend whose mind is all over the place and his ADHD is sometimes in overdrive. He has a hard time focusing on what someone is saying if he is preoccupied and cannot do two things at once. It's possible to ask him as many as three times to do something—and he may even agree. But once it's time to act, it's as if he is hearing the information for the first time. One time he agreed three times earlier to take his daughter to an event, but on the day of the event he had not allowed enough time in his schedule to take her because it was farther than the location he thought he'd heard. He was frustrated, and she was mad and confused. Instead of resolving to listen better, he defensively told her he would just say no to her request next time. True, that would reduce confusion, but clearly it's not the right course of action.

So, what can you do to take the right action before it's too late? The next few chapters will explore 11 ways to identify blind spots and various options for you to see where you may be falling short in the key areas and relationships that mean the most to you. The first four strategies include:

1. Look for Patterns
2. Beware of Strengths Taken Too Far
3. Get Connected
4. Receive Feedback Openly

Let's begin by looking at these strategies to help you find your blind spots—and do something about them!

1. Look for Patterns

My (Ashley) father bought my mother a car early in their marriage, and at some point the "check oil" light appeared on the dashboard. My mother, who knew nothing about cars, failed to take note of that indicator and ignored it. It eventually caused quite a bit of damage to the whole engine! Sometimes there are dashboard indicators in our life, trying to warn us about a problem we should act on. These indicators are often visible in the form of patterns. As you read the following ways to identify blind spots, look for patterns in your behaviors and in outcomes. Do you go from job to job without learning what you may be contributing to the problem? Have you had similar disagreements with different friends repeatedly?

When you see a pattern beginning to develop in your life, you should look at it like an indicator on your dashboard. It might not be anything serious, but you'd be crazy to ignore it.

One time, a friend of mine (Brian) called me on the phone to catch up. We talked for a while and then he told me about three odd interactions he'd had while running errands that day. "It must be a stressful time for people today," he said, confessing that three people at three separate venues had become annoyed with him "for no reason." I listened to the three scenarios and then realized there was a pattern. In each case it was a female associate in a retail store, and he was the other common variable. I encouraged him to probe deeper and see what he might have done to provoke their frustration. "How did you contribute to that problem?" I asked. He thought a minute and quickly discovered that his friendly and playful demeanor was not well received when others were busy with many customers waiting behind him. This conversation opened up a window of opportunity to discover other situations where his upbeat attitude (which is normally a strength) was having diminishing returns.

I've seen several people that I call the "two-yearers." (I know that's not a real word, but it's my phrase.) These people will work at a place for about two years, get fired or quit, have a season of unemployment, and then find another job. This pattern repeats itself time after time. In every instance that I have observed, it brings great pain to key relationships, especially marriages. Sometimes there are extenuating circumstances, and there are no blind spots responsible for the outcome. But often there are early signs: poor communication patterns, over-inflated egos, and even the seedlings of depression that can be recognized and dealt with, eliminating cyclical stress that can wreak havoc on a career and families. Identifying patterns early and addressing them can change the trajectory of one's life, often avoiding some catastrophic failures.

Another pattern that is worth watching for is when events happen to you uniquely. If you've said, "Can you believe it happened to me *again*?"—for the fourth time in a month—there might be something there.

Not every pattern is bad. For example, perhaps you are asked to give your opinion consistently at meetings, or neighbors always ask you to watch their house. These would be indicators that people value your insights and that you develop trust well.

Maybe you've found that while you have the same level of education and experience as colleagues, you're getting passed up for promotions. What are the other factors that are present? Perhaps there is a specific skill that you need to develop to be considered for a position. At one of our recent trainings on Coaching for Performance, a woman shared how she aspired to become a department leader in her organization. She had developed the relationships necessary to be noticed. She was also in the final stage of getting the appropriate certifications for the position. But nothing had happened so far.

As we considered the role she wanted and her current skill set, we found a gap in her communication skills. This was a problem because she would need to conduct presentations for large groups on a quarterly basis in the new role. These speaking opportunities were critical for the success of the company, and it was imperative that the department leader have at least a solid ability to present, if not mastery-level presentation skills. However, she confessed that it was public knowledge in the organization how much she despised getting up in front of groups, and she avoided it at all costs.

She had not made the connection that she was not going to be seriously considered for that position until she addressed her fears, grew her skills, and changed how people perceived her desire and ability to lead presentations. We were able to identify her distinct learning style and how she could gain the skills and confidence needed and then demonstrate it to the appropriate people to set her up for the desired position.

The next strategy for identifying a blind spot might surprise you. We all have strengths. Most of the time these strengths work for us. However, it is possible for our strengths to be taken too far, go un-checked, and work against us.

2. Beware of Strengths Taken Too Far

Early in my (Ashley) career, the director of my department exhibited symptoms of a strength taken too far. Jan was blunt and her knack for candid commentary was appreciated. She entered the department during a time of vast change. We were hungry for clear ideas and an ability to make decisions. Jan fit the bill. She was honest about the issues and changes facing the department and was great at making the difficult call. We trusted her decisions.

After a few years, the changes were deeply integrated into the culture of the department. Our path was clear, and we were well-poised to stay on track and meet our goals. Jan, however, didn't change her leadership style in reaction to our current needs and environment. During department meetings, Jan would boldly declare what we should do and how we should do it. That worked well during the chaos of change, but people didn't like being bossed around during a time of clarity. Jan's strength worked well in one environment and was taken too far in another. Because she was not able to identify that this strength was taken too far, she did not adapt and she was soon seen as stubborn, loud, and difficult.

Had she changed into that type of person? No, her strength remained the same…it just wasn't effective because it was too strong in this different environment. Good leaders not only know themselves, but they also know what environments and situations play to their strengths and when they need to adapt or allow others to take the lead.

Other examples of strengths that are often taken too far include:

- Humor—Sometimes a jokester is a great comic relief, and sometimes they are inappropriate or annoying.
- Congeniality—Most of us like working with nice people, unless they are so nice that they cannot speak their opinion or give corrective feedback for fear of hurting others' feelings.
- Chattiness—In elementary schools, students used to receive marks on report cards for talking too much. The workplace doesn't give out report cards, but too much chatting is a problem for everyone. Communication is important, and being a communicator is mostly a strength—unless the person doesn't know when to stop communicating!

In *Strengths Based Leadership*, New York Times bestselling author Tom Rath reveals the results of decades of research. The book focuses on three critical elements to be a more effective leader: 1) knowing your own strengths and investing in the strengths of others; 2) getting the right people with the right strengths on your team; and 3) being mindful of and meeting the four basic needs of those who look to you for leadership. He writes:

> *All too often, leaders are blind to the obvious when it comes to something of critical importance to them—their own personality. Many political and business leaders have self-concepts that are miles away from reality. They simply don't know their own strengths and weaknesses. This is the stuff of parody for late-night talk shows, sitcoms, movies, and stand-up comics. And this problem goes far beyond the boss who thinks he's funny, even though people only laugh at his jokes out of obligation. Most people have encountered a leader who is completely unaware of a glaring weakness. We have spoken with several leaders who claim to be great at developing their people, but when we interview the people they lead, we hear a very different story. In some cases, the leaders in question may be better at demoralizing than developing people. At its worst, this lack of self-awareness can lead to masses of disengaged employees, unhappy customers, and undue stress beyond the workplace. Although less noticeable, another serious problem occurs when people try to lead while having no clue about their natural strengths.*

The benefits of discovering your blind spots can be great for your career, your colleagues, your organization, your family, your overall well-being, and much more. However, you have to want to find them. You have to search as if for hidden treasure…and then be courageous to consistently address the issues you uncover. For many of us, this is best done by partnering with others in a micro-community of trust and growth. That's the point of the next strategy: getting connected with others. The more time we spend with others, the more opportunities for awareness we will have about ourselves and others—assuming we pay attention to the verbal and non-verbal feedback we receive.

3. Get Connected

If you want to learn more about yourself, spend time with a lot of different people in a variety of situations. Join activities both in and out of your comfort zone. As you interact with people, you will not only learn about them but also about yourself! Often people who have lingering blind spots do not spend a lot of time connecting with others.

We're both big fans of the sitcom *Seinfeld*. While it ran on television from 1989 to 1998, the creation of Jerry Seinfeld and Larry David lives on through reruns, quotes, and endless clips. In one episode, Elaine and George are at an office party. The music starts, but no one is dancing. While George is off getting finger food, Elaine shouts out, "Alright, who's dancing? Want me to get it started?"

She proceeds to hit the dance floor as all the guests look on…in disgust. As George turns around and sees her, he exclaims, "Sweet fancy Moses!" The scene transitions then into a dialogue between Jerry and George.

"Elaine danced?" Jerry asks.

George replies, "It's more like a full body dry heave set to music."

"Did she do the little kicks and the thumbs?" Jerry inquires.

"What, you mean you know about this?" says George.

Jerry goes on to share about a situation that occurred five years earlier when a reggae band was playing on the streets of New York and Elaine started dancing. Cue the flashback. The looks of annoyance from everyone but Elaine are very similar to the faces from the office party. Jerry had hoped that it would go away on its own by now. George wraps it up with, "Sometimes you can't help these people until they hit rock bottom!"

While it would have been great if Elaine would have learned the lesson earlier…we certainly would have missed the comedic genius of this favorite episode! The reality is that we've got to be the kind of friends, family, and colleagues who don't wait until people hit rock bottom if we want the best for them. Unlike Elaine, we must pick up on the signals and suggestions that we're getting, which is the next point. There are a variety of ways that you can do that as you'll see in the next strategy, but in most instances you just have to ask for feedback and be willing to receive it.

4. Receive Feedback Openly

At Core Insights, we make it a habit to glean feedback after significant events. If we're presenting on a new topic, speaking to a new audience, or rolling out a new training activity, we're going to invite feedback on it. Because we ask for feedback, and it is received with an attitude of openness and willingness to change, we receive quality information that impacts the overall delivery and success. When you combine an environment of trust, an element of vulnerability, appropriate timing, and thoughtful communication, great discoveries await you.

In our business, quality feedback leads to greater impact on the people, businesses, and non-profits that we serve. Here are some of our best ideas for building a better feedback loop—all learned through experience:

Build your feedback team.

Recruit a small group of people you can trust and that you know will share openly the good and the bad with you. You don't want a bunch of "yes men" in this brigade; you want people who will shoot straight and ask hard questions to help you refine what you're doing—whether it's a sales pitch, an email to correct an employee, or the way you handled a customer on the phone. Also keep in mind that your feedback team will likely need to change over time. As your roles and relationships change, reevaluate the people in your life serving as your feedback team.

You may be called upon to be part of someone else's feedback loop. In 2016 Core Insights became the representative for Dale Carnegie and Associates in our region of Texas. One of the foundational concepts of this internationally-respected organization is how to share feedback with others. The first step, they say, is always to start with the **evidence**. Then they recommend that you move to discover a suggested **action** the person can take. And then share at least one solid **benefit** if the person takes action.

You might say something like, "Here's the evidence of the problem I see…here's the action I'd suggest you take…and here's at least one benefit you will receive if you take action…" This is a valuable pattern to follow as you share with one another in your feedback team.

In some situations, people are unwilling to take action on the information they receive. This is usually because they believe the feedback they are getting is either incorrect, unimportant, an isolated viewpoint, or something they cannot change. In other situations, it's the team that's unwilling to give feedback. After speaking at an event on a college campus recently, a student asked a great question. He shared, and I would concur, that many times when we ask for feedback, people are reluctant to share openly and honestly about items that need to be corrected. What do you do then?

My response was two-fold. First, I think we get better feedback if we carefully phrase the request. I often use this approach: "I am really seeking to do the best that I can, so what is *one* thing that I can do differently to make [this presentation] more effective?" You'll have to tweak the phrasing to fit your situation, but by demonstrating you're willing to improve, not just fishing for compliments, you're more likely to get useful and applicable information.

Second, as people increasingly see us not being defensive when we receive the feedback, they are more willing to give it. They see how we use their opinions in helpful ways, make necessary changes, and demonstrate our appreciation for their candor—and that means they'll be far more likely to share helpful feedback the next time, whether we ask for it or not!

I've (Brian) seen this truth in action within my family life, in the workplace, and even with people who regularly attend some of our sessions. Case in point. After one recent training, a client that we work with regularly shared with us a powerful video that illustrated one of our points in a very effective way. We were delighted! She knows that we put a lot of time, energy, and research into our presentations and that when we're delivering the training we're very focused on connecting with the audience and making it applicable. She also recognizes that we're very open to ideas and suggestions and constantly seek to grow and improve. Over time, the barrier of wavering between, "Should I say something?" or "Will they take this the wrong way?" has been removed and she's become part of our regular feedback team!

Develop a formal 360-degree feedback process.

Despite the fact that our company provides this tool for clients, I (Brian) have often gone outside of my colleagues and peers to be sure that I get an unbiased opinion of how I'm doing professionally and personally. In an effective 360-degree feedback process, you select a variety of people, including those who report to you, peers, superiors, customers, people you volunteer with, a spouse, and others in order to give you a well-rounded and more complete view of how you are doing and how you are perceived. Typically, you use a well-deliberated survey to gather information. Then, depending upon the level of commitment and investment, the facilitator (that may be you or someone else you choose) may conduct interviews to gather more information. After that, you process the survey results and interview data so you can see both your strengths and weaknesses. Every time I go through this process, I learn things about myself. Sometimes people see strengths that I wasn't aware of, but at other times I realize I'm not being perceived the way I want to be, and I take steps to remedy the situation.

Hire a mentor or a coach.

By sharing with a life coach or mentor about situations and outcomes, you can ask key questions that often bring additional areas to light. Having a coach observe you in various situations or in areas that you know are challenging for you, but you don't know why, can be a great asset.

I (Brian) was once coaching a gentleman who was struggling with communication regarding a critical business partner. We decided that I would sit in on a meeting as a consultant. As I observed the meeting, I discovered a host of items my client could work on to make that relationship and communication stronger. For example, the environment of the meeting could have been set up to provide a more collaborative spirit. Preparing a simple agenda could have ensured they were both focused on the same items and moving forward together. At several points, my client loudly and forcibly said, "No!" when a clarifying question would have been far more appropriate. In addition, there were several non-verbal leaks, such as a furrowed brow, that came across the wrong way. We'll discuss deciphering non-verbal cues later in the book.

As my client and I recapped the meeting later, I asked questions to debrief the experience. My client had *no idea* that he was coming across so harshly to an ally that was vital to his success. He made corrections that drastically improved their interaction.

In their next meeting, my client sent an agenda a few days before their meeting and asked for input on the outline for their time together. They met in a conference room that allowed them to sit in a more collaborative fashion, versus across from each other. My client chose his words more carefully and asked more questions. I checked back a few months later. In addition to the above items, they were occasionally scheduling a time to walk various properties and discuss issues. Their relationship had improved and the business referrals had too.

Sometimes people may share feedback with you and they *don't* have your best interest at heart. But you can still glean from it. The historic account of a Jewish leader named Nehemiah is an example. He was in charge of rebuilding the walls around ancient Jerusalem. He received information from allies, friends—and his enemies. He simply determined what was true and could be beneficial—regardless of the source—and from those insights he reshaped his plan. His leadership brought great benefit to his people as a result.

Ask good questions.

Sometimes the best thing you can do is ask pertinent questions and listen to the answers. Ask your feedback group, "What seems to matter most to me right now?" If you led a presentation or a meeting, afterward ask questions like, "What stood out to you? How do you think the group perceived me? What's one thing I could do better in that situation? What should I make sure to continue to do in that environment?" These are all questions that can help you to dig down and find treasures about your skill set and personality that are buried beneath the surface. It's all about helping you to find those blind spots in your life.

More Ways to Find Out More

In our experience, we've discovered 11 different strategies you can employ to identify your blind spots. You're now familiar with the first four. In the next chapter, we'll unpack four more ways to identify what hidden strengths and weaknesses you can address in order to become even more effective. This next set of strategies deals with your ability to learn, your character, your non-verbal communication styles, and behavioral styles that impact your everyday living.

o   o   o

Personal Reflection

- Can you remember a time when you saw a destructive pattern and made a change in your behavior? Explain.

- What do you consider to be your greatest strengths? Why?

- Is it easier for you to connect with others for personal growth at work or home? Why?

- Who should you connect with to build your feedback team? When will you connect with them?

- On a scale of 1–10 (10 being the "most open" and 1 "not open at all"), how open are you to feedback typically?

- What can you do to demonstrate to others that you want feedback?

Group Discussion

■ Are there any patterns in your life that came to mind as you read this chapter? What might those patterns be telling you?

■ Take turns and have people share the strengths they see in each other. Then, have each person share a corresponding potential danger for some of the strengths that were mentioned.

■ Share the connections you have that can or could provide you insights into your blind spots.

■ What could we do to create an even greater sense of trust, leading to asking and answering questions more openly?

■ Share with the group one action step you're going to take this week to demonstrate a greater desire for feedback.

CHAPTER 6

Take a Good, Hard Look. Repeat.

When you change the way you look at things,
the things you look at change.
Max Planck

If you're like me (Brian), the number of tools I have in my garage have grown significantly over the years. When I was 22 and fresh out of college, I had a small tool kit and one saw. If you were to go into my garage today, you'd see hanging on peg boards four different types of saws and a plethora of other tools. I can choose the right tool for the job now! If I'm cutting a tree limb, I have a couple of different options to choose from, and I'll consider the situation based on my choices. Sometimes what I initially try doesn't work and I'll head back to my "arsenal" and make another selection. Similarly, we want to give you multiple strategies for your blind spots toolbox because you may need to address the issues from a number of angles. Here are four more strategies to add to your toolbox when you're trying to improve your performance at work and in life.

5. Become a Lifelong Learner
6. Watch Out for Character Issues
7. Study Non-Verbal Communication
8. Understand Behavioral Styles

5. Become a Lifelong Learner

We all know them—the dreaded know-it-alls. Some of us tolerate them with a good dose of patience, and others cannot stand to be around them. Urban Dictionary defines a know-it-all as "one who makes it appear as if they're an expert on a subject while there are also signals (subtly or blatantly noticeable) that this person doesn't know very much on the subject or at least not as much as they're acting like they do on the subject." Know-it-all people tend not to listen to others' ideas or consider alternate opinions because they feel their own is superior.

When it comes to understanding the ins and outs of your unique personality, gifts, and challenges, it's impossible to be a know-it-all. There will never come a time when you will take care of all the blind spots. Instead, the goal is to be a lifelong learner. This is a person who has developed the ability to challenge themselves and also has the desire and motivation to change along the way.

Lifelong learners keep evolving as they go through life, mindful and observant of how others respond to them. They stay busy evaluating and integrating helpful feedback. If you *want* to change, you can change. You can't fix all of your blind spots—that's unrealistic. The fun is in the improving and becoming a better version of yourself with every passing year. You'll also discover that, depending on what stage you are at in life, your blind spots change over time. So, there's always a challenge ahead if you're keeping your eyes open.

The next strategy for uncovering a blind spot is to evaluate your character—who you are when no one is looking.

6. Watch Out for Character Issues

Character issues often sneak up on you without your even realizing it. A blind spot often starts small and grows into a problem. You may have heard this poem:

> *Plant a thought and reap a word;*
> *plant a word and reap an action;*
> *plant an action and reap a habit;*
> *plant a habit and reap a character;*
> *plant a character and reap a destiny.*
>
> *-Bishop Beckwaith, 1885*

Often the person does not even recognize they are drifting from their desired goals. They may not realize a problem even exists. In the book *Mission Drift* authors Peter Greer and Chris Horst explain the process of an organization's slow drift from its original mission. Usually, this happens over a period of time, so the drift may not even be realized until the problem is significant.

One of our (Ashley) favorite family pastimes is boating, and we have seen firsthand the problem of a slow drift. One time our neighbor was out on the lake with her three small children when they decided to jump in and cool off in the water. One of her children remained on the boat as the mom and other two kids swam around. Within moments, the mother noticed that the boat was getting farther away from her. She decided it was time to swim back to the boat, but the more she swam, the farther away the boat drifted! She quickly realized she was not going to be able to catch up to the swiftly drifting boat. The child on the boat began to panic. It was more than 30 minutes before a passing boat found the stranded swimmers, and by that time their boat had drifted almost out of site. The experience was very traumatic for the entire family. In fact, they sold their boat and have not been on the lake since that incident.

These drifts can also happen to individuals' character without their realizing what's happening. Look out for common examples of character deficiencies that develop over time like lying, gossiping, and complaining. At first, it's just telling a small "untruth" or making an "innocent" comment that does not line up with your core values. But over time, when these habits continue, they become an issue of character.

The next strategy is paying attention to non-verbal cues that people may be giving you regarding a particular flaw you have.

7. Study Non-Verbal Communication

I'll (Brian) never forget how the world of non-verbal communication opened up to me. A close friend of mine from Chicago had sent me some interesting information that he had discovered on non-verbal communication. I kept the material in my car for several months, just waiting for the opportunity when I had some uninterrupted time to read over it.

I had to drive to an iconic East Texas barbeque restaurant one day for a board meeting, but I was not sure how to get there. Uncertain how long it would take or the amount of traffic I would face, I allowed extra time. I arrived at the meeting early, so I sat in the parking lot and started reading the material from my friend.

What I discovered was fascinating.

Many years later, I still remember being astonished at what I read about the power of non-verbal communication and wondering how I had missed this fundamental aspect of communication for so long.

But I was also a little unsure about some of the specific

information and was curious how accurate it was. I was about one-quarter of the way through the content when it was time to go in for the start of the board meeting. I went in the restaurant, ready to apply some of my novel discoveries. I immediately saw someone I knew could influence my business, but I had not yet made a connection with him. I asked if the seat next to him was available, sat down, and began drawing on the insights I'd just read about non-verbal communication. Remember, I was skeptical. But I proceeded to position myself in such a way that communicated my interest and enthusiasm in a more impactful way than mere words. I made sure my body language, facial expressions, and the way I positioned my chair all signaled, "I really want to hear more about what's important to you." I also read his body language and responded appropriately. We had a great interaction that day and I thought to myself, "This information on non-verbal communication is legit!" This is how my foray into reaping the rewards of non-verbal communication began, and it's been a fascinating journey that continues to this day.

Understanding non-verbal communication is a priceless spotlight highlighting areas that we might otherwise never see. We're devoting extra time on this one strategy alone—it's that important. I have used all of the following techniques over the years to help me to see more of what someone is communicating to me through their body language. What is your body language communicating?

Eight Non-Verbal Signals to Watch for

The following eight non-verbal signals can help you to see what people are *really* saying to you. These messages don't come through the lips. They can reinforce what a person says, adding more flavor to the message. But in other instances, these non-verbal cues and clues contradict the intended message. These eight basic non-verbal indications reflect raw, automatic emotions and responses and are often uncontrolled. We give and receive vital information to others by our: proximity, relative orientation, facial expressions, touch, eye contact, gestures, inflection, and use of adaptors. Let's walk through each one.

Proximity is a good indication of the level to which we are liked or people are interested in what we are saying. Let's say someone you know well walks into a room during a mixer, but every time you get near them they duck into another part of the room like a groundhog on the prairie. You should at least be conscious that there may be an issue between you.

On the other end of the spectrum, some people walk into a room and come right over to you. Their decision to have greater proximity with you should help you to realize that you've made a connection. We need to be careful about what story we are telling ourselves, but the lack of proximity with people should at least lead to questions like:

Did I put too strong of a sales pitch on them the last time I saw them?

Did I fail to properly acknowledge a gift?

Did I cross the line and tell an embarrassing story the last time we were together?

Be mindful here and don't take it too far. We can misinterpret circumstances and be guilty of telling ourselves negative stories that aren't true (e.g., "people aren't interested in my stories" or "they don't enjoy my presence").

Relative orientation is the way we position our bodies when we are relating with someone. Typically, we directly face people and items that interest us or that we like. The next time you are at a gathering of people, observe the way people position their bodies when they are talking. You're likely to find that when people become disinterested in a specific subject, their shoulders shift and their focus and gaze will turn. What are people's posture when they are talking with or listening to you? Do you unintentionally signal disinterest or boredom with those around you?

Facial expressions communicate a lot of information to others, even when we are not intentionally displaying an expression. Upon starting a new career several years ago, I (Brian) was introduced to a coworker who had a very angry facial expression most of the time. Whenever we attended meetings together, I began to feel very self-conscious when speaking in front of Rhonda. When I was talking, her already negative facial expression would turn to what I interpreted as disgust. I immediately began to wonder: "Does she disagree with my ideas? Does she dislike me? Does she think I was the wrong hire? Why does she look so disgusted?" I asked a trusted peer if perhaps something about me was upsetting Rhonda. What I found out was shocking. Rhonda's facial expression had nothing to do with me. I was simply seeing the expression she makes when she is thinking, my friend explained. Rhonda obviously needs to spend some time observing her facial expressions and make an effort to change to a more positive disposition!

The primary facial expressions are happiness, anger, sadness, fear, surprise, and disgust, and they are typically very similar across cultures. We can train ourselves to focus on facial expressions at pivotal points in conversation with others and learn to decode them to glean critical information. Facial expressions trigger automatically whenever we experience an emotion. When we are angry, for example, our face shows our anger with our furrowed brow, red cheeks, etc. While we're conditioned to try to hide these expressions, they still involuntarily occur for one-fifth of a second…even when we're fighting to hold them back. We may even try to manipulate our facial expression to convey an emotion we don't really feel. Smiles are one of the most faked expressions. A real smile uses the muscles around the lips *and* around the eyes. An insincere smile only uses the muscles around the lips.

I recall when I said something to a prized intern and quickly became concerned that it may have been taken the wrong way. I had just wrapped up a meeting and made a statement to him that seemed to be innocuous enough. As I said it, however, I picked up on an ultra-brief facial expression that clued me in that I may have offended him. We left the meeting, each got into our cars, and drove away. As I processed that exchange over the next few minutes, I decided it would be best to follow up on the non-verbal cue that he neither intended to share nor likely even knew that he gave. I called him on his cell phone and began, "I think I may have said something that could have been interpreted the wrong way. Let me clarify what I was trying to say…" He listened and then let me know that he *did*, in fact, think that I was saying something else, and he was really glad I called! We were soon back on the same page.

Over the years, as I've interviewed candidates for job positions, I've benefitted from the discipline of watching people's expressions at critical junctures of the interview. If what they say does not match with the micro-expression they're demonstrating, then I usually ask follow-up questions until I'm comfortable that I understand what caused the disconnect.

Physical touch is another non-verbal expression. We can say and learn a lot through physical touch. We throw in a caveat here that we are talking about appropriate physical touch and not unwanted, unsolicited, or inappropriate touch. An appropriate touch includes extending a handshake and offering a pat on the back. Physical contact is often meant to convey a desire to connect, a way to get another's attention, a feeling of comfort and familiarity, or to demonstrate closeness. Rarely will you find someone reaching out for physical contact without there being a connection with the other person. Conversely, if you find someone resisting an appropriate gesture, it may be an indication that you don't have the relationship that you thought you did or that you have done something to wrong this person.

Eye contact is another indication of someone's true feelings. Much like other non-verbal cues, it can be a great barometer of interest and liking. We tend to look longer at things that have our interest and attention. However, we have a tendency to limit our eye contact when we are socially anxious, shy, embarrassed, ashamed, sad, or trying to hide something. Failure to make eye contact can also indicate that we don't want to talk to another person.

It's good to look for patterns when people are unwilling to make eye contact. On more than one occasion, a lack of eye contact during a one-on-one meeting has helped me to realize someone's discomfort. It suddenly occurs to me that they mistakenly think I've called them into a meeting because they're in trouble! So, I take steps to make the environment of our meeting more relaxed and comfortable, on par with the relaxed business conversation I want to have.

At other times, I've recognized a lack of eye contact in a discussion has nothing to do with me or our conversation. When I follow-up with a phone call or email, I usually find out that the other person is going through a challenging time and needs help.

I've also experienced times where lack of eye contact has clued me in to the fact that I've offended someone. Limited eye contact can also be something as benign as a sign that someone is thinking about a complex answer or trying to remember something. Be sure to consider the whole picture before you draw a conclusion.

Gestures Unlike facial expressions, gestures have varied interpretations in different cultures. More than anything, gestures can help you discern the other person's passion for the topic at hand. If you don't believe it, try sitting on your hands when you are conveying something to someone on a topic that you really care about. How does it feel? By the same token, if someone is not utilizing gestures, then it's possible they don't have strong opinions about the topic. All of this is key information for you to take in, evaluate, and apply to your benefit when you are in a work environment. How does someone on your team respond to the new project you've assigned them? You thought they would love it, but their gestures and other indicators tell a different story about their lack of passion.

Inflection One's voice is a treasure trove of information as we seek to look for blind spots in our lives. Like a barrel with holes, we "leak" a tone and rapidity in our voice that can help us to discern emotions, stress, and anxiety—in ourselves and in others. We may talk faster and at a higher pitch when we're nervous or excited, for example.

Recently, I (Brian) was part of a small group of business leaders and heard the president of a significant institution make a presentation. Having been around this president on numerous occasions, I was keenly aware that something was different in this setting because I could hear in his voice numerous revelations of discomfort. Excessive use of fillers or disturbances like "um" and "ah," changing the direction of the sentence, or excessive repetition can also indicate some level of discomfort with the conversation. If you pick up on these clues, ask yourself: "How am I adding pressure to the situation? Have I created an unfriendly environment? Is the person unprepared? What other stressor is present?"

Adaptors The use of adaptors can also provide you with great clues that others are bored with or stressed by what you are saying. Adaptors are those things that we start to fidget with when the situation is uncomfortable or boring. You may observe coworkers playing with their hair, spinning a pencil like retired television host David Letterman, or clicking their pen. These are great indicators that something is going on beneath the surface that we should be aware of.

Notice if and when these habits appear in specific presentations, certain topics, particular meetings, or with certain people. And pay attention if you're the offender! Recently, I caught myself playing with my keys in a meeting, telegraphing: "I'm ready to get out of here." I didn't mean to do it, and I promptly stopped and put my keys far away from me. But it reminded me to be keenly aware of not only the messages I receive but also the ones I'm giving.

8. Understand Behavioral Styles

Sarah was in one of our Core Insights trainings when she experienced exactly what we aim for: an "aha moment." In the middle of the half-day program, she pushed back her chair from the table, smiled, and exclaimed loud enough for everyone to hear: "Now I get it! Now I understand why I'm so worn out at the end of every day!"

Sarah was a well-educated counselor, guiding people through the various challenges they face in their lives. Despite having a master's degree in her field, she'd failed to recognize some key elements in her own life. In our program on behavioral styles, she discovered not only her natural style of effectiveness but also the unnatural ways she was performing that were draining away her energy. Sarah is highly relational on the behavioral scale (we'll explain more later) and is energized by positive interaction with people. She had done a very good job in her role as a counselor, truly believing that she could make a difference in people's lives. She had even been promoted to a supervisor's position. However, Sarah soon found herself spending more time with paperwork, administrative tasks, and correcting staff who routinely showed up late, had poor attitudes, or weren't very caring toward their clients. This new role took a significant toll on her, and it was impacting every facet of her life.

Like Sarah, when we are aware of our preferred behavioral style, we get a much more accurate view of how we uniquely view the world. We see how we are similar to and different from others. To discover a person's unique behavioral style, we utilize the Workplace Insights© tool (available on our website) and have been using it regularly for 30 years. We've found this tool to be statistically accurate and helpful at a cost-effective rate. There are numerous tools available, including Myers-Briggs, DiSC Profile, and Colors, but this one works best for us.

We produce a report that accurately describes your distinct habitual patterns of thought, behavior, emotion, and communication. It provides objective insights and action steps regarding your unique strengths, including a narrative explanation of the four scales used to measure your four natural strengths:

- Problem Solving
- Processing Information
- Managing Change
- Facing Risk

We briefly address these four behavioral areas next. Just being aware of these elements has proven to be pivotal for so many people in both our trainings and coaching experiences. For more information, go to **www.CoreInsightsLeadership.com**.

Problem Solving – On one end of the continuum are the people who like a challenge and appreciate a fast pace. They gravitate toward acting upon problems. Conversely, on the other end are those who are not motivated by a challenge and prefer a slower pace. They prefer time for reflecting on issues and deliberating a course of action.

Processing Information – This scale focuses on how people naturally see situations. Some people are typically optimistic and prefer to see things more positively. Those who are on the other end of this scale are more realistic and less trusting, often seeing what can go wrong. Additionally, those who are more optimistic usually gravitate to higher levels of people interaction and a faster pace.

Managing Change – This scale focuses significantly on the amount of consistency a person is attracted to. On one end of the continuum, people like a very predictable and systematic pattern and are typically not very emotional or expressive. On the other end of the scale are the people who are emotional and expressive. They crave change and are very excitable.

Facing Risk – This measurement focuses largely on the degree to which someone desires to be precise and orderly, following or establishing rules and procedures. On one end of the spectrum are people who are very conservative. They usually have a greater sense of fear and are typically risk averse. Others at the opposite end of the scale could be portrayed as having no fear and as being more tolerable of a high level of risk. At our trainings on this subject, I (Brian) often ask the question, "If you were choosing an accountant to prepare your taxes, where would you want them to fall on the continuum?" After receiving some feedback, I usually encourage them to choose an accountant who leans towards the accurate and meticulous side...unless they've always wanted to do time in a federal prison!

How Behavior Influences Blind Spots

Armed with this basic understanding of the various styles, let's talk specifically about common blind spots for each of the styles and how strengths have corresponding weaknesses. This is only a cursory review, and we'd suggest that you dig deeper into this topic if you've not yet explored your own behavioral style.

Those who are more aggressive in Problem Solving are often so direct and fast-paced that they offend and "run over" people without even being aware of this tendency. If they do not keep this behavior in check or "tame it," they will be perceived as pushy, impatient, domineering, tough, and harsh. Conversely, those who are more reflective can sometimes be wrongly perceived as passive or uninterested.

When it comes to Processing Information, those who are naturally optimistic and people-oriented can sometimes be seen as disorganized, undisciplined, manipulative, reactive, or vain. Therefore, it's important for them to put systems into place in order to be more organized. It's helpful for them to remember that sometimes confrontation is necessary and that thinking critically is important. On the flipside, those who are more realistic need to be conscious that defaulting to a "What's the worst that can happen?" mindset can produce great value but also be harmful to their personal brand because they're perceived as "Debbie Downer"!

They need to know when and how to present negative information.

Those who gravitate toward predictability on the Managing Change scale typically like to take their time and contemplate. Doing this in excess, or doing so in every situation, can lead to inaccurately being perceived as unsure, insecure, awkward, conforming, and wishy-washy. People who score high in this area can grow by being more expressive when listening and speaking and making faster decisions on items of a less critical nature. On the other end of this continuum are those who are more comfortable with change. They're often described as dynamic and often need to give others more advance notice and not be as spontaneous when others' schedules are involved.

Those who have a need for more structure when it comes to Facing Risk make up the smallest percentage of the population. They need to learn to adapt to various situations, instead of defaulting to only their natural style (which leads others to consider them picky, critical, judgmental, fearful of criticism, and slow to make decisions). The phrase "paralysis by analysis" can often be ascribed to this group. On the other end of this continuum are people who often don't observe rules or norms and cause stress to established systems and procedures.

We all have a natural way that we approach situations, events, and people, along with a default style of communication. And yet it's important that we learn to adapt to situations, versus having a "That's just not me!" attitude.

When we increasingly recognize our uniqueness and are conscious of the strengths, weaknesses, and opportunities for growth in all of the behavioral styles, then we are far more likely to detect blind spots that are inherent with each one. Keep in mind that there are great strengths to each and every aspect of these four scales. However, if we don't maintain an awareness of the corresponding weaknesses, and we don't understand the differences between individuals, we will hamper our own effectiveness!

Introducing Emotional Intelligence to the Equation

The final three strategies in the next chapter focus on the importance of knowing your level of emotional intelligence, as opposed to just your IQ. They will challenge you to try something new and to take time to understand yourself on a different level. Once you understand all 11 strategies, you'll be able to mix and match to uncover your weaknesses and get to work on these areas.

o   o   o

Personal Reflection

- What have you learned lately that makes you better at your role at work?

- How do you learn best?

- What is an area that you've not explored that would be helpful for you to learn more about?

- Are there any character issues that you've relaxed on or not held to the same standards that you have in the past? Why?

- What surprised you the most about the section on non-verbal communication?

- Take some time to speculate on the behavioral styles of the three people you spend the most time with each week. What evidence can you give for your choice?

Group Discussion

- What is the most helpful thing you've learned in the last five years? What impact did it make?

- In what environment can you use a greater understanding of non-verbal communication in the coming week? What are some possible outcomes?

- Describe your behavioral style to the group.

- Who in the group shares similarities? Where are there more significant differences in behavioral styles among us?

- How can these differences help us to identify blind spots for each other?

CHAPTER 7

How Intelligent Are You?

Information is not knowledge.

Albert Einstein

I (Brian) recently got a new tennis racquet and simultaneously discovered that our local university was hosting a community tennis night every Tuesday evening. While I've played tennis for nearly 40 years and was even a college tennis coach back in the day, this opportunity brought new life to a sport I've enjoyed since I was a kid. I meet up with new friends I enjoy being with, not to mention I am becoming a better player by sharpening my skills. How are you doing so far in your efforts to improve in a specific area of your life? You may have worked in the same field, lived in the same city, and spent time doing the same things for many years, but we hope you're discovering that these strategies have the potential to bring new life into your old routines. All of these strategies are valuable to use in your quest to be the best version of you wherever you live, work, play, and volunteer by learning to fine-tune your work performance and elevate your key relationships. Let's discover the remaining three strategies for detecting your blind spots:

9. Know Your Emotional Intelligence

10. Try Something New

11. Study Yourself

9. Know Your Emotional Intelligence

Emotional Intelligence (EI) refers to the ability to recognize, regulate, and evaluate one's own and others' emotions.[2] It includes how well a person can perform three basic steps:

1. Identifying Emotions: First, emotions must be accurately perceived. This requires understanding body language, facial expressions, and tone of voice, as we learned in the previous chapter.

2. Decoding Emotions: The emotions that we perceive can carry a wide variety of meanings. If someone is expressing a sad emotion, we must decode the cause of the sadness. It might mean a sad event recently occurred, or perhaps they are simply tired and being perceived as sad.

3. Managing Emotions: Regulating personal emotions and responding appropriately to others' emotions are important aspects of emotional management.

Research began nearly a century ago on new topics such as social intelligence, emotional strength, and multiple intelligences. These concepts were the forerunners of what we know today as EI, a term that was coined in 1985. It's not necessary to read a lot of research, however, to understand the three basic principles of how EI works in everyday life:

1. Some people are better at reading others' emotions.

2. People who can read others' emotions well and react

appropriately fare better in social situations.

3. People who can control their own emotions well are easier to spend time with.

When my (Ashley) oldest son was a toddler, we spent a lot of time at the local park and pool. We wanted to socialize him and ensure he had plenty of opportunities to interact with others and make friends. I remember a specific instance when we were sitting in the sandbox with my son and several other children and parents. My chubby little two-year-old was walking around meeting the other children by telling them his name and asking for their name. He was not shy and was very verbal. Another parent commented, "He's going to be a great politician one day."

I reveled in the great job that we had done in teaching him the social skills needed to be successful. Fast-forward 10 years. My son is now a preteen, and while his IQ is quite high, his EI is quite low. He is still very skilled in shaking hands and meeting new people, but he is often inept at reading others' emotions, responding appropriately to those emotions, and controlling his own emotions.

On Father's Day this year, we decided to write fun messages to my husband in white shoe polish on the windows of his car. On the way out to the garage, I asked my son about a documentary he watched on television the night before. Big mistake. He went on and on for 20 minutes detailing the show. Despite my non-verbal communication signals (no nodding, continuing to complete the task, interrupting with task-related questions, no eye contact, etc.), he continued to talk. How could he not see that I was not interested in that long of a monologue? He does not read emotional and social cues well. It's a blind spot for him and many other people like him. People whose EI is low often have blind spots related to relationships and social norms. They may not "fit in" well in various social settings and may even annoy people.[3]

There is some disagreement on whether having EI (or the lack of) is something you're born with or if people can learn skills that raise their EI. Personally, based on my own observations, I believe that some people are born with a high EI and others are not. I also believe that people can learn skills that will increase their EI. We have been working on this for years with my son. When it's obvious that he is blind to the verbal and non-verbal cues he is receiving, we point them out to him and help direct him to respond appropriately. We are seeing progress, and it takes persistence and consistency.

10. Try Something New

I (Ashley) can clearly remember sitting in Mrs. Cole's second-grade class, listening to her share details about a University Interscholastic League (UIL) competition on Storytelling. Students listened to a storyteller read a brief story and then had to retell the story in their own words before a judge(s).

I sat quietly at my desk, listening to my teacher read the competition requirements. I waited, desperately hoping that someone would answer her plea for a volunteer to compete. Silence took over the room, and I could see the disappointment on Mrs. Cole's face. I was, and still am, a "people pleaser." It pained me to see our beloved teacher's hope fade that a student would take on the challenge. When I could stand it no longer, I raised my hand to volunteer.

My peers and teacher stared at me in disbelief. Even I was surprised by this bold move! It wasn't so much that they were surprised that someone had finally volunteered; it was because the most shy, quiet kid in second grade had stepped forward. As I mentioned earlier, I was silent with others, outside of a few close relatives and family friends. You can imagine my mother's shock when she read the note saying that I would need to stay after school for UIL practice. I assumed that I would fail. Public speaking just wasn't in my DNA. I was far too shy to even say hello to neighbors who waved as I rode my bike down the sidewalk. How was I going to compete in a competition that required me to tell a story to complete strangers?

It's funny how one decision can change the course of your life. No one could believe it when I brought home a first-place ribbon in Storytelling. It wasn't just a fluke; I continued to bring home first-, second-, and third-place ribbons for years to come in Storytelling, Oral Reading, Duet Acting, and One-Act-Play. Competing in UIL events was only the beginning. I went on to study communication in college and graduate school and decided to enter the training and development world upon graduation. Today I regularly train, facilitate, and speak to groups large and small. Who would have thought that the shy kid in second grade would one day be a public speaker by trade?

This all began with a choice to try something new, even though it seemed way out of my league. I'm not promising that if you try something new you will discover a strength that will become your dream career. You will, however, learn some things about yourself. Trying something outside of your normal behavior gives you new perspective on yourself. You may discover hidden strengths, or you may discover something that is holding you back from success. Self-discovery doesn't usually just show up at your doorstep. It requires you to get out of your comfort zone and try something that you haven't done before.

So, what can you try that is new?

If you have the self-confidence, you may be ready to try something big like a new hobby, sport, volunteer role, or even a job change. If you need to start more slowly, consider a small change such as meeting someone new for lunch or even trying a new recipe. With each experience, take time to assess what you learned about yourself through the process. There is truth in the old Chinese proverb, "Pearls don't lie on the seashore. If you want one, you must dive for it."

This summer, I (Brian), had a few problems with various pieces of equipment at both home and work. Some of them were minor, such as an extension cord for lawn equipment that quit working. Some of them required taking additional steps, like repairing telescoping pieces and the wheels on my luggage. My lawnmower even died in the middle of mowing the lawn. I found myself increasingly wanting to repair these items personally, rather than buying into the disposable mentality that permeates our society or automatically engaging a professional.

What I discovered after a few successes was that I was much more likely to give it "the old college try" (with some help from the Internet) and that success breeds success…minus the lawnmower. It proved to be too much even for the professionals and was destined for the lawn equipment graveyard.

Similarly, the compounding effect of identifying and addressing our blind spots will reap rewards as well. The more we do it, the more it becomes very natural to do.

11. Study Yourself

In addition to the numerous ways we've already discussed, there are two questioning techniques that will help you study yourself to gain more information about current challenges and opportunities facing you.

Ask Tough Questions

Ask yourself tough questions that require you to identify what role you have played in a specific situation—the times when things are going exactly how you want them to and the times when nothing is going your way.

A friend of mine (Ashley) was recently laid off after about 18 months on the job. Alli is a very intelligent and creative executive who had a lot to offer the small business where she worked. The company was facing numerous problems. Even though work conditions were less than ideal, as a single mom she needed the job. As we shared a cup of coffee one day, I listened to Alli tell me about all of the problems with her ex-employer. She was angry and hurt and needed some time to grieve and vent.

Within a few weeks, we met again and Alli had secured another job. I then decided to help her spend some time studying herself as she reflected on all that had happened. So, I asked her some tough questions to prompt her thinking. The conversation went something like this:

Ashley: Alli, I know your last employer had a lot of issues.

Alli: Yes, maybe it was actually a blessing that I was laid off.

Ashley: As you are moving into your new role, it may be beneficial to reflect on your last job and determine if there are any lessons learned that you should work through to be even more successful at your new company.

Alli: Well, I hadn't even considered that I would need to do that since the reasons the company was failing were so obvious. I wasn't that surprised when they laid me off. They couldn't afford to keep me with the company in such a bad state.

Ashley: Yes, the company was obviously under financial stress. In your role you could have been helping with the issues, hurting the issues, or doing both. It's worth at least considering these possibilities. Doing so may give you some great insight that you will find beneficial in your new job.

Alli: Okay, what do you suggest?

Ashley: Let's start at the highest level. Related to your layoff, what role did you play in that happening?

Now, let me forewarn you. The initial response that I got was not very insightful. Alli restated all of the problems with the company and the owners, and she drew the conclusion that those issues were the cause of the layoff. I took note of each issue. Then, I asked the same question, "What role did you play in that?" about each of the stated issues.

It took some digging, and I had to ask quite a few second-level questions to draw out information that was helpful to Alli. In the end, she realized that she had become disengaged after an incident that occurred months earlier when one of the owners had questioned an important decision she had made. The more the problems mounted, the more disengaged she had become. Alli then realized that she could have been more proactive to help solve the company's problems. She even admitted that she now recognizes a pattern in her behavior. When things aren't going well, she tends to step aside and let the storm blow in. Now that she knows she has this tendency, she can be aware of it and put steps in place to handle future situations better.

Think about a recent disappointment you experienced at work. The following questions are ones you can ponder to process that experience and learn about yourself:

- Was the outcome what I expected? Better? Worse?
- Why was the outcome different from or the same as what I expected?
- What was my role in the situation?
- How did I contribute to the outcome?
- What could I have done to improve the situation?

Walk through the "5 Whys"
Another proven technique you can use to problem-solve any unexpected or disappointing outcomes in important situations is the "5 Whys." This questioning technique was originally developed by

Sakichi Toyota and was used within the Toyota Motor Corporation during the evolution of its manufacturing methodologies.

The technique includes asking the question "Why?" five times, each time building on the answer provided by the previous question. Here's an example of how I (Ashley) use it. Let's say you present a great idea during a staff meeting, but the team does not seem excited about your idea. You scan the room, but there are no significant signals in your coworkers' non-verbal communication. Nobody is saying anything that gives you additional ideas on why your idea didn't resonate. The meeting adjourns and you walk back to your office in a bit of a funk.

Ask yourself "why" five times in a row and answer yourself honestly.

1. Why did the outcome not go as planned?
   I didn't have time to fully explain the real benefits of my idea.
2. Why?
   I took too long sharing background information on how I developed the idea.
3. Why?
   Often people in that meeting tend to not really listen and take ideas seriously.
4. Why?
   There are so many crazy ideas presented in these meetings and rarely is any action taken.
5. Why?
   The meeting is really used for brainstorming and not for making final decisions on processes. There is no formal agenda, and people consider this meeting a waste of time.

Aha! You have found the root cause!

The reason the team was not excited about the idea had nothing to do with the idea itself. The lack of structure and the informal purpose of the meeting was the likely issue. Now you can pause and strategize when and where is the right place to present this idea again—and how to do it. Instead of misappropriating the blame to yourself (our self-talk is often wrong), you can regroup and prepare.

Asking "5 Whys" is usually enough to get to the root cause of an issue, but more or fewer questions can be used. In this case, one more question might drive you to see that you don't often strategically consider how to communicate with your team. Asking questions will prompt you to study yourself carefully. When that happens, you are likely to find blind spots.

What Will You Do Now?

Now you know all 11 strategies. If you have used, or are using, some or all of the methods we've introduced to you, then celebrate! You have taken a huge step forward in identifying a great opportunity to improve your personal or professional situation. So, what are you going to do with that knowledge? Will you take action or go back to ignoring the problem? In the next chapter, we'll show you what's likely holding you back from springing into action and also give you advice on the concrete steps you can take right now to reach your goals.

∘   ∘   ∘

Personal Reflection

- Which of the methods you learned in this chapter do you already naturally use to identify blind spots?

- Which of the methods were unfamiliar to you?

- Try something new every week for the next four weeks that will push you out of your comfort zone. What insights did you discover about yourself?

- Use the "5 Whys" technique to find the root cause of a problem or issue at work. Then ask, "What can I learn about myself, now that I better understand why the issue occurred?"

Group Discussion

- What insight stood out to you most from this chapter?

- How could we be more strategic in each other's lives to identify blind spots?

- What would help this group develop a stronger level of trust?

- What 2–3 questions could we ask each other in the coming months to help identify blind spots? (Reminder: Blind spots can hide both positive and negative issues.)

CHAPTER 8

Excuses, Excuses

He who refuses to embrace a unique opportunity
loses the prize as surely as if he had failed.
William James

I (Brian) grew up in Oklahoma. While there are many great benefits to growing up in Oklahoma, accurate pronunciation of many words is not one of them. Combine that with being married to a teacher who is willing to remind me of my wayward diction and living with teenagers who snicker at my occasional poor expression of the English language, and you realize that I have people drawing attention to one of my blind spots! Among other faulty enunciations, it was pointed out to me one day that the days of the week end in "d-a-y." Proper pronunciation is "day," versus Sundee, Mondee, Tuesdee, etc. Since I speak to groups all over the country, I worked on it pretty diligently and effectively until I changed the way I say the days of the week.

I once shared this story at a conference to illustrate a point, and an astute participant came up afterwards and pointed out that according to the dictionary it was acceptable in some regions of the country to say "dee"! Still, I've tried to keep the "day" instead of the "dee"!

What motivates us to change our blind spots is very important. I was motivated to change in order to be more professional in my job. What motivates you?

World War II produced some significant changes in American lives for very specific reasons. People were pulled off of farms to live in urban areas and provide labor for war industries. Working married women surpassed the number of working single women for the first time. African Americans and Hispanics moved to war industry-rich areas, increasing racial tensions. Even fashion changed, as people needed convenient clothing options to fit the changing demands of their work and personal lives.

Why were people during World War II so willing to undergo massive change? Because there was a sense of urgency. The war directly affected the American way of life. People sensed the need for teamwork in order to defeat the imminent threat. When people are faced with a serious situation, they are much more likely to change.

During a recent discussion with the president of a financial services firm, he confessed his communication skills were lacking. He became aware of this fact several years ago when he was appointed to be the president, a role that requires him to be a true leader in the company. Not only is he responsible for numbers and results but also for building a team. In our coaching relationship, I (Brian) asked him if he had taken steps to improve his communication with employees. He said he had not. When I asked why, he said that things were running smoothly, and the team seemed to be functioning quite well, despite his difficulty in communicating with them.

The problem, however, was that things had recently taken a turn. Some tenured employees had left, and some new employees had joined. "Suddenly" the team dynamics were hindering productivity and morale. He knew that if he didn't do something quickly, there would be more turnover and customers would be negatively impacted. The situation was now an emergency! He had to take action or the organization might not survive. He knew there was an issue long ago, but he wasn't ready to address it until the situation was dire.

Thankfully, he actively worked on his communication skills and even took a Dale Carnegie course called High Impact Presentations. For a season, he regularly strategized with me on board meetings and important memos. I sat in on a couple of meetings with his staff and a key stakeholder. He examined many facets of his communication, and in the end, he turned the situation around. But, he lamented, how much better it would have been if he'd addressed the identified blind spot earlier.

When there is not a state of emergency, people are much less likely to take action. It is easier to live another hour, another day, another week, or another year in your current state unless there is a really compelling emergency looming. People usually have a specific reason for why they don't take action upon blind spots they know they have. Based on our experience, their excuse is usually tied to one or more of the following: lack of motivation, pride, complacency, fear, and selfishness. Let's unpack each one and see which one(s) may be holding you back from taking needed action.

Excuse Number One: Lack of Motivation

What motivates you? The answer to this question is unique to you. What motivates one person may not move you at all. People are often motivated by things like:

- Reputation
- Relationships
- Success

- Money
- Achievement
- Recognition
- Meaningful work
- Responsibility

How do you know what motivates you? Spend some time thinking about a time when you felt really energized doing something. This will likely give you some significant clues to your source of motivation if you'll probe your memory. Consider using the 5 Whys technique. Here's the first "why": Why do I feel motivated to do _____?

Several months ago, an acquaintance of mine (Ashley) packed up her dilapidated minivan with some belongings and her three children and left an abusive relationship. She didn't know where she was going or how she would provide for her kids. I was very motivated to put her in touch with resources that could help her. I even enlisted help from my circle of friends to provide some immediate needs. For about a week, I spent much of my personal time making phone calls to coordinate assistance. I sometimes kept her children so she could search for a place to live and find a job, and I spent many hours listening to her concerns. As the urgent needs were met, I was able to reduce my support and enjoy watching her build a new life for her family. My husband commented that he could not remember a time when I was as energized as I was while I was helping her. I agreed. I felt inspired! As I thought about other similar situations in my past, I realized a trend. My energy level and motivation to act is clearly connected to helping others.

Think about situations in your past that motivated and energized you. Write each situation and take the time to jot some insights to process what exactly it was about these situations that motivated you.

Once you know what drives you, you can turn that into a question that will motivate you to take action. Whenever I encounter a blind spot, I try to tie it to what I already know motivates me— helping others. I ask myself, "How will taking action on this blind spot *help other people?*" Once I answer that question, I can feel the motivation to act welling up inside of me.

You can do the same. When you discover a blind spot, think about how taking action on it will tap into your most effective motivation. For example, "How will taking action on this blind spot *increase my salary potential?*" Or "How will taking action on this blind spot *help me feel more confident?*"

What trends do you see? When you find your motivation, and you make appropriate changes, you'll see a greater impact on what matters most to you. When you see that impact, you'll be increasingly inclined to look for and address your blind spots because of past successes.

Excuse Number Two: Pride

Pride is generally considered to be a positive emotion. It is associated with satisfaction, success, improved self-esteem, and a feeling of belonging. When pride is on the line, people are motivated to go above and beyond to reach a goal. We often hear phrases like "Take pride in your work" and "Have pride in your organization." Pride isn't always positive though. Sometimes pride can be taken too far and become destructive. Proverbs 16:18 states, "Pride goes before destruction, and a haughty spirit before a fall."

Hubristic pride is another example of a strength taken too far and involves arrogance and entitlement. The word *hubris* came from the ancient Greeks and referred to mortal beings who believed they were superior to the gods. They felt special and therefore believed they did not have to follow the rules outlined by society.

On Friday, February 19, 2010, professional golfer Tiger Woods stood before about 40 selected guests and delivered a televised press release apologizing for extramarital affairs. His admission garnered immense negative publicity and cost him millions of dollars in commercial sponsorships. Tiger's own words detailed how his success led to hubristic pride that spiraled into a dangerous sense of entitlement. According to the transcript of the meeting, he said, "I knew my actions were wrong, but I convinced myself that normal rules did not apply. I never thought about who I was hurting… I thought I could get away with whatever I wanted to. I felt that I had worked hard my entire life and deserved to enjoy all the temptations around me. I felt I was entitled. Thanks to money and fame, I didn't have to go far to find them. I was wrong. I was foolish. I don't get to play by different rules. The same boundaries that apply to everyone apply to me. I brought this shame upon myself."[4]

It's not just sports legends who can get lured by hubristic pride. A sense of entitlement can breed in any environment and is often harmful to others. Sometimes when a blind spot is identified, pride takes over and the person feels that taking action will indicate failure. Therefore, they are unwilling to act upon the problem.

In our work with companies all over the country, we consistently see that employees are looking for leaders who are authentic and humble—and willing to admit when they are wrong. Whether you're in a position of leadership now or not, develop the willingness to fight back your pride.

Excuse Number Three: Complacency

"Things are pretty good right now. Why should I change anything?" This is a question that many people ask themselves (although they may not admit it) when they discover a blind spot. You may sometimes hear people on a diet say, "Losing the last 10 pounds is always the hardest." Is that really true? Or is the reality that once we get so close to a goal we become complacent? After all, we're more fit than we were and our clothes fit better than they did, so things seem pretty good. Why work so hard and push to follow through to the end?

Similar feelings happen in other aspects of our personal and professional lives too. If we are fairly happy with the situation as-is, then we may not feel an urgent need to take action. Be on your guard against complacency! Aim for the best, not just the better.

Excuse Number Four: Fear

One of professional boxer Mike Tyson's early trainers was Teddy Atlas. Atlas writes a lot about fear in his book *Atlas: From the Streets to the Ring—A Son's Struggle to Become a Man.* He points out that fear usually lasts longer than the thing you fear. In boxing, it takes less than a second for a boxer to get in a tough hit, but boxers spend countless hours and days fearful of that hit. The buildup of fear is often more excruciating than the actual physical pain that occurs. So, why do people spend so much energy squandering their time with fearful thoughts? Why do we get stuck in a state of fear and therefore not progress to taking action?

Fear is a pre-programmed protective mechanism to increase our chance of survival. Fear of being hurt can be helpful in keeping us from running off a huge cliff or climbing a tall tree. Fear only becomes debilitating when we don't take risks even when the potential of a positive outcome outweighs any possible negative return. If you find yourself not acting on something you need to change about yourself due to fear, ask, "What is the worst that could happen?" Write a list of possible negative outcomes. Then, ask yourself, "What is the best that could happen?" Write a list of possible positive outcomes. Study your two lists carefully. Do the potential benefits outweigh the risks? Are the possible negative outcomes really that detrimental? Often our fears prove to be unfounded. When we take a systematic approach to overcoming those fears, we free ourselves to try new things.

Excuse Number Five: Selfishness

We've seen it over and over again. In learning something detrimental about themselves, people often make an excuse and say, "Well, that's just the way I am." Sometimes they even take it a step further and state, "Everyone is just going to have to deal with it." This is one of the great fallacies of human nature; that we cannot change and therefore others must "get used to it." What a selfish view!

Many years ago I (Brian) knew an employee who often made comments in an accusatory manner. For example, if a coworker was a note-taker and found value in taking notes during team meetings, this person would ask in a snappish tone, "Why do you waste all that time taking notes?" Several people on the team approached me with similar examples that had resulted in hurt feelings and damaged relationships. I met with the employee and shared how his comments were impacting the team. He was shocked and had no idea that he was offending others. That is a classic blind spot. However, then he said that his coworkers were obviously too sensitive and that they were going to need to "toughen up" a bit. I could tell that his selfish view was filtering his perception of the situation.

Guess what? People don't have to deal with you just because it's the way you are. In this employee's situation, I ended up removing him from the team because of the damage he was doing to our culture. If you ever find yourself thinking or saying, "That's just the way I am…," stop and recognize that the statement isn't really true. Everyone should be willing to change.

Ways to Increase Your Willingness to Take Action

If you have discovered a blind spot and are not sure if or how you will do anything about it, try some of the following activities to test your willingness to change. Doing so can make you more open to taking the right steps toward improvement.

1. Ask yourself, "Why should I take action?" and then write the reasons why you should do so. If you clearly understand why you are taking action, it will be more appealing to you and you will be more motivated to act.

2. Similarly, make a list of the pros and cons to taking action and then compare the two lists. Do the pros outweigh the cons?

3. Just start with something. Sometimes getting started is the hardest part of being motivated to take action. Even if you are not sure that you are taking the correct action, do something. Once you get moving, the actions you need to take usually become clear.

4. Set goals and write them down. What actions do you want to take and by when? Put them on your calendar for added accountability.

5. Enlist the help of a partner. Find someone who will motivate you and hold you accountable. The person you choose can be a coach, mentor, coworker, friend, or relative, as long as they are honest with you and have your best interest in mind.

6. Read related books or articles to get new ideas and put your brain in motion. This technique especially helps if you are stuck and are not sure how to get started. Find a book related to the topic you are interested in working on and find actionable ideas. More on this in the next chapter.

7. Develop a mantra for yourself. A mantra is a statement about what you want to do and why you want to do it. For example, if you have found that you often talk over others and risk being perceived as a poor listener, your mantra

may be something like, "Slow down and take time to listen fully." It may even help to think of a cheerleader yelling this mantra to the crowd, loud and with a striking cadence: "Slow down! Take time! Fully listen!" When you are in conversation with others, state your mantra to yourself when you feel the need to speak before others have finished speaking.

8. Celebrate successes! When you reach your goals, celebrate! Building upon your success can keep you inspired to continue, so celebrate each step of the way. This may mean you pause to reflect on the progress that you've made. It may also mean taking a break from work and going for a walk on a beautiful day or running to a local coffee shop for your favorite drink. If you really hit a great milestone, go out for a steak lunch. You get to choose how you mark the occasion, but do celebrate!

It's Up to You

You are the only one who can decide to take effective action in your life. You have to be willing to learn, grow, and change to become the person you want to be. Our hope is that that you've now identified a blind spot and you're ready to take action. A certain level of research into the issue will serve you well, rather than jumping into action. We'll explain why in the next chapter—so don't skip this step and risk being guilty of what one friend calls, "Ready, Fire, Aim." Think about that for a moment. In the next chapter, we'll show you how to take the time to aim before you shoot! You'll discover how to snoop around like a private investigator to find additional information, research the topic, and discover resources that might help you go to the next level.

o   o   o

Personal Reflection

Walk through the following set of questions for each blind spot that you are considering working on. Write your answers in a journal and review them often.

Blind Spot Action Plan

Blind Spot #1:_____

- Why is it worth dealing with?

- What are the pros of taking action and the cons of not taking action?

- Now list as many options as possible for potential actions you could take to deal with your blind spot.
    1.
    2.
    3.

- Who could you enlist to help you?

- What resources should you utilize?

- How will you know if you're successful?

For more sample sets of questions, turn to Appendix B for a blank Blind Spot Action Plan.

Group Discussion

- Share what blind spot(s) you've identified thus far and why they are worth addressing.

- How does what others think of you impact your motivation to address your blind spot?

- In the past, what has kept you from taking action on items that have thwarted your success?

CHAPTER 9

Taking Effective Action

*Even when opportunity knocks, a man still has
to get up off his seat and open the door.*
Anonymous

My (Brian) youngest daughter went through a season, a long season, where she would get "hurt" often. It wasn't long before this became pretty obnoxious for the entire family. Since being hurt is subjective, it was hard to tell her that she wasn't really hurt. I had conversations with her that began with questions like, "What does hurt mean to you?" and "Do you realize how many times a day you say you're hurt?" But I didn't really see any behavior change.

I decided that I would help her see how often she mentioned personal pain and cause a little disruption to her life too. Every time she shared about pain or injuries or used words like "ouch" and "hurt," she had to go into my office at home and write on a specific tablet the date, time, and description of what happened. It wasn't long before she shared with me that she had "realized" that she really does talk about minor wounds and injuries "a bit much."

Some of these incidents were legitimate, but many of her complaints were the byproduct of some bad habits where she overreacted. She was unaware of this until she personally saw the pattern and her life was disrupted by having to chronicle each incident. She got tired of stopping what she was doing or getting off the couch to document her discomfort. It changed her behavior...and the Brandt family rejoiced!

Take the First Steps

We suggest taking a multifaceted approach to get rid of a blind spot in your life. It involves getting information, testing your new behavior or change, evaluating the results, and getting input or accountability from a third party. You may find a wealth of resources on the topic via the Internet, a good book, or a training program that will help you remedy the situation.

We were recently leading a session where a young lady came in late, drawing our attention to her. She had a very inviting smile that permeated her persona for the entirety of the session. I (Brian) admired the way she carried herself. The following day, I was on a video conference call where I observed my own default facial expression. While it wasn't a scowl, it was far from the friendly guise I had seen the day before! I determined that this was a blind spot I wanted to improve upon. I had seen a great model, recognized an area for improvement, and then determined to make a change.

Here's the plan that I developed:

SAMPLE PLAN for a Warmer Persona:
1. Identify the desired behavior, which in this case is to present a friendlier face.
2. Tell a colleague my plan, as she is in many meetings and trainings with me. Ask for accountability and help to remember to smile more when appropriate.

3. Draw a smiley face on sticky notes and place them in some key spots (by my computer monitor and on my iPad) to remind myself to smile.

4. Put smiley faces on my calendar to remind me to smile in meetings I was headed to.

5. Ask for input from a few people who demonstrate the behavior I want.

6. Schedule a time to video myself in three different scenarios and evaluate my expression.

7. Set up an incentive plan for myself. (My favorite ice cream treat if...)

8. Make a point to smile even when nobody is around.

9. Walk around airports and malls with a big smile on my face.

10. Listen to comedians when driving or doing chores at my house.

It wasn't long before I started to get some very positive reactions to the friendlier persona I created. I liked the results, so I kept going with the action items longer than I had planned. Guess what? It became a habit. (It's worth noting that as I reread this section months later while editing this book, I realized that I had regressed. The sticky notes are back up around my office, as I seek to reclaim this aspect of my life again.)

Additionally, some people have found they can benefit by studying those with similar issues via books, case studies, lectures, biographies, or documentaries. It helps to see how others have positively overcome the issue and how they are reaping the benefits of a changed life. At other times a good biography might provide a cautionary tale about *not* addressing the issue. In 2013, the movie *Jobs* debuted in 2,300 theaters across the country. Hundreds of thousands were able to see the brilliance of Steve Jobs who has brought us such devices as the iPod, iPhone, and iPad. But they also saw the portrayal of a man who left a wake of sour relationships behind him. Use the successes and challenges of others to change your life for the better. Eleanor Roosevelt said, "Learn from the mistakes of others. You can't live long enough to make them all yourself."

Ingredients of Successful Action Plans

My (Brian) family is a big fan of the popular show NCIS (Naval Criminal Investigative Service). We've watched this team of special agents solve countless murders in a mere 40 minutes. I wish we could effectively deal with our blind spots in that time. In order to truly correct what has been thwarting our best potential, it takes the skill to identify a problem, the willingness to change, and the courage to take deliberate steps. Let's break down the key ingredients of successful action so you can pick your methods, make your plan, engage others, and execute with gusto.

Make an Apology

One of the main characters in NCIS named Gibbs has a long set of rules that he and his underlings strive to live by. Number six on the list is "Never apologize. It's a sign of weakness." He's not the first actor to project that ideal. John Wayne, a legendary tough guy in Westerns, followed the same mindset. It may work on TV, but it doesn't usually serve us well in the process of making a change. If the blind spot we have discovered has an obvious negative effect on others, an apology can provide a multitude of benefits. First, it establishes a stake in the ground for us and others that this behavior we've identified in ourselves is not acceptable. Subconsciously, and maybe even consciously, we will then desire to avoid repeating the behavior and having to apologize again. An apology often gives us greater accountability, opening the door to frank conversations if this behavior returns.

Get Accountable

Accountability can be a powerful tool in our efforts to correct our blind spots. Whether it's poor listening skills, not managing our time well, or always being negative, it helps to have someone holding us accountable to making strides towards improvement and correction.

Over the years, I've (Brian) found a few critical elements to effective accountability relationships. Consistency and commitment are pivotal. You must be prepared to connect with your accountability partner on a regular basis. Harder still, you must demonstrate commitment to not only be present but also to be vulnerable.

Openness and honesty are other key ingredients of accountability—if you truly want to see a difference in your life. Otherwise, you're just wasting your time and that of your accountability partner. At times, it can be advantageous to agree to have your accountability partner check-in with a coworker, spouse, someone who attended one of your meetings or presentations, or even a key vendor to get their perspective on your progress. With many accountability relationships, there is a temptation to focus only on avoiding actions or attitudes that are harmful. However, I've found that the best accountability includes a goal-oriented and proactive approach toward a better situation. For example, if you find yourself talking too much in meetings, don't stop at holding your tongue. Make it a goal to listen more attentively, take notes of key points, and contribute to better post-meeting follow-up.

Engage a Coach

Engaging with a coach can produce a great return on one's investment. For many people, the financial cost alone of not remedying a blind spot can be significant. Many have found the consequences of their blind spots to be a costly lack of productivity in their department, failure to obtain a key contract, a lack of promotion, not getting a position that corresponds to their education or experience, or even a divorce.

While the initial sticker shock of the cost of a qualified coach might prove paralyzing, it may be exactly what you need to make the necessary changes. An effective coach will understand the problem clearly, digging deeper to be certain that it's the real root issue. From that foundation, a coach will typically suggest resources and action steps to get results. Then, they'll interact with you on what is going well and what needs to be tweaked to get you to the desired point.

While we at Core Insights coach many executives, we've found no two situations to be exactly alike. Coaching relationships are as unique as the individuals...and snowflakes. In one recent situation, we were brought in to coach two key employees who would not cooperate with each other. One woman, who was very task-oriented and great at her sales job in the oil field industry, was not willing to "walk on eggshells" around a coworker who supported her in the sales process. Likewise, the other party sought to receive a "reasonable amount of respect" and not be steamrolled in their interactions. As is often the case, the truth was somewhere in the middle, but neither could see how they were contributing to the issue.

Acting as a mediator, I (Brian) was able to create scenarios and identify how each could work together to accomplish the organizational objectives, while acting civilly to one another. In one of the quickest victories I've ever seen in a coaching relationship, they swiftly realized that they were very unaware of how different their behavioral styles were. They were then able to minimize what they described as "stepping on each other's toes by 8:15 each morning." Over time, they even learned that their differences actually complemented each other well in their environment, and they gained great advantages by working together.

Look for a Mentor

Similar to a coach, a mentor can be a powerful force in rectifying a blind spot. At age 30, I (Brian) had become the C.E.O./Executive Director of a regional non-profit that needed a turnaround. The board found themselves with over a million dollars in debt, dwindling demand and impact for five years straight, and a disappointing drop in staff morale. The board made it very clear that rectifying these issues should be my marching orders, and I was excited about moving from Missouri to Texas and taking on this new challenge.

As I settled into my role, I realized that overall we had a good team. We delivered a great product to the families, churches, and schools we served. I began to work on the turnaround, and at the end of two and a half years, our team had delivered and the board was thrilled with the results. The debt had been paid off, we had waiting lists for our programs, and the staff of approximately 150 was engaged and excited about our mission. As I began to contemplate the next season, a longtime mentor and friend asked me to be part of a dot-com startup. Meanwhile, the next vision and plan had stalled with the board. I wanted a new challenge, so I moved on to the next chapter in my life.

It was only years later, as I worked on my master's degree in Global Leadership, that I discovered a blind spot in my leadership capabilities. While I had some of the best role modeling in servant leadership, I had not had much role modeling in the area of planning and envisioning the long-term future. Or at least I had not availed myself of it if it was there. Nevertheless, I had neither recognized the need nor studied it. It was truly a blind spot in my leadership model.

Once I became aware of this missing critical component, I

looked around for a mentor to help me with this area of weakness. Fortunately, I found a willing mentor in Dr. Scott Lawrence. Having grown up in the home of an Army general, graduating from the Air Force Academy, and being a Top-Gun fighter pilot-turned-medical doctor, he was quite the strategic thinker. I asked if he would mentor me in this area, as well as in others, and he agreed.

Over the course of the next couple of years, he questioned my thinking; we read books and discussed them; we trained others together; we developed a leadership program for our church; and we led a temporary shelter for Hurricane Katrina evacuees. This life-on-life approach focused on my blind spot, and it made a profound difference in my life.

In the ensuing years, it was always humorous to me how often people pointed to the strategic thinking that I had provided for different organizations, not knowing that it was only a recently acquired asset! For the first 35 years, it had been an unknown weakness. But like a surgeon removing a tumor, this destructive blind spot had been removed from my life, and in its place was a treasure that had been hidden for years. Once uncovered, my knack for strategic thinking began benefitting not only me but also many organizations and individuals because I was able to provide highly strategic insights. A mentor helped make that happen for me.

Get the Real Picture

Many of our clients ask us to help them with their public speaking and presenting abilities. We've trained all kinds of people—some days before they were interviewed for *60 Minutes*, some in preparation for securing a seat on the city council, and some prior to speaking engagements in the nation's capital. Sometimes they just want to be more effective with daily inner-office meetings.

Several relevant components of our trainings deliver what

they're looking for. In most scenarios, we video a client and allow them to see how they really come across. In some instances, they find they're a far better communicator than they thought. At other times, they see themselves using mannerisms they were completely unaware of! It's exciting to see them get an accurate perception of their abilities.

We then role-play the environment where they will speak. This allows them to envision what it will feel like, what might go through their mind, and what pressures they will face. One of the "homework" assignments we recommend is to watch other speakers, noting both positive and negative elements of their messages. The website www.TED.com and the accompanying app are both great tools to find an aggregate of speakers on a wide range of topics. While the topics are interesting and potentially beneficial, it's what our clients learn while observing the speakers' delivery that often serves them well.

What could you do to observe yourself and others regarding your identified blind spot? How can you use technology to your benefit?

Practice Makes Perfect

In Appendix C, we've included a list of Common Blind Spots and Suggested Actions as a worksheet for you to complete using the skills you've acquired in this book. Take some time to walk through these issues—you can use it for your own benefit or to benefit someone else. We've included some examples to get you started.

In the final chapter, we've detailed several real-life stories to encourage you as you begin the work of coaching yourself to the next stage of success. Some are cautionary tales, and some will inspire you to take that next step.

○   ○   ○

Personal Reflection

By now, you have hopefully developed options for a plan of attack regarding one or more blind spots. Now, determine your path and set out on it, one step at a time. Reread your action plan for dealing with blind spots in Appendix B and answer the following:

- Study your list of possible options you could take. What actions will you definitely take?

- What is the timeline for those actions?

- Study your list of resources. What resources will you need for each action?

- Study your list of names for enlisting people to help. Who are you going to engage and how?

Group Discussion

Each group member should reference the Blind Spot Action Plan and tell the members about the implementation of his or her plan. Have each member make 1 or 2 observations about the plan as it's presented. Then have the group ask each member follow-up questions:

- What surprised you as you worked your plan?

- What tweaks in your plan do you think you should make?

- What is motivating you to continue?

- What successes are you seeing so far?

CHAPTER 10

Making It Stick

There are no secrets to success. It is the result of
preparation, hard work, and learning from failure.

Colin Powell

Within weeks of wrapping up this book, my (Brian) wife paid me the nicest compliment. She said, "I will say, when an issue for improvement is shared with you, you absolutely take it to heart and work on it." I was glad to hear it because I do take seriously the matters that have been brought up by my family—from changing mispronunciations that had become commonplace to eliminating phrases that were hurtful to others. I've even trimmed my eyebrows and changed some bad eating habits! Remember, people are much more apt to share with you the areas they see need improvement the more you positively respond to their feedback.

If you've made it this far in the book, you've likely grown in your ability to address the blind spots that you've discovered. But the process isn't over. There are a few additional steps to ensure the changes you make will be permanent.

Evaluate the Outcome

Once you start seeing positive results in various facets of your life because of your hard work regarding one or more blind spots, take a time out. Evaluate the situation, the requisite actions that you've taken, and the results thus far to determine if you're achieving the outcomes you desired.

For example, consider if you've really taken all of the steps needed, learned all the lessons that you need in order to make sustainable change, and fully changed the habits that you wanted to change. Evaluating the process this way will give you even more motivation and confidence to repeat it. Determining if your outcomes match your desires will be different for each blind spot. You will want to go back and review the clues that led you to discover the issue in the first place and then determine if those clues are still applicable.

As another example, if you were being passed up for new job opportunities, are you still missing out now that you have acted on one or more blind spots? If you started watching your sarcastic tone with your family, are you seeing improvements in those relationships? Or are you still finding yourself being really sarcastic to family members, even after you've recognized that's a pattern that causes stress in your relationships? These are the tough questions you have to ask yourself.

Repeat the Process Often

Evaluation is important. And so is repetition. New blind spots come at different stages and with different circumstances. If you're already putting into practice what you've learned from us, you've likely developed some tools, including a great feedback team, that will help you to quickly discover other issues—hopefully before you lose ground or miss another opportunity.

It's a little like the instructions on the back of a shampoo bottle (as if you needed those instructions). *Wash, rinse, repeat.* Seek to use the tools that we've discussed, like watching non-verbal cues and observing patterns in your attitudes and actions. Work to have such great rapport with people that they regularly seek the best for you and know that they can communicate their concerns in such a way that these discussions are welcome and not stressful. When you do this repeatedly, you truly can grow into a cycle of continuous growth and improvement.

We recently added a new member to our training team at Core Insights, and we were especially mindful to demonstrate our core value of seeking feedback as soon as possible after an important event. After three of us led a training together at a Fortune 350 company, we sat down over lunch and debriefed various aspects of the presentation. We considered the design, execution, engagement, and delivery of each of the trainers. Even though two of us were long-seasoned trainers, we demonstrated to our colleague a genuine desire to look at what we could do better. I've (Brian) made it a long-standing practice to ask the question, "What's one thing I could do better to make that training (or speech) more effective?" Stay at it—repeat the process of working on your weaknesses—and it will get easier and you will get better.

Learn from Others' Mistakes

Evaluate. Repeat the process. Take time to learn from the mistakes of others. We saved these cautionary tales solicited from our survey to remind you of the importance of the task you're undertaking.

In 2007 I began working at a new company whose workforce was 100% women. My coworkers welcomed me with open arms. I was invited to lunches and afternoon Diet Coke breaks and participated in hallway chit chat. I was beginning to really like this place, and I was fitting in to the office culture, or so I thought. Soon I noticed that I wasn't being invited to lunch as often. I wasn't offered the opportunity to have a quick beverage break with my new friends. In fact, even most hallway pleasantries ceased as well. I began to wonder what I had done to fall out of the good graces of my new coworkers.

I thought that I was helpful, focused, conscientious, and excelled at my work. In fact, I learned a long time ago that the best way for me to work was in an area not affected by office pollution (i.e., office chatter, noise from a radio, or even a cluttered office). When the office pollution was too much for me to be able to focus on my work, I simply shut my office door. I thought that I was doing the right thing. I didn't want to hurt anyone's feelings by asking them to be quiet so I could concentrate. It was their office too. I didn't want to come off as being the new diva in the office.

I thought that I was the perfect coworker, so why was I being shunned? I began to ask the couple of friends that I had retained at my new office why my social interactions with my coworkers had come to a screeching halt. The feedback—I had given the impression that I did not want to interact with my coworkers because I consistently had my door closed. My need for a quiet environment to work in was not communicated. What I mistakenly communicated was that I was a snob.

What was my remedy? I wanted lunches and Diet Coke breaks and hallway banter. I wanted to be a good coworker. I simply had an informal conversation with those who thought I was a snob. I apologized for giving the wrong impression and told them of my optimal work environment. My relationships were restored, and I once again received invitations to lunch and Diet Coke breaks!

From that point forward when I felt the need to omit the office pollution, I would simply say, "I'm closing the door. I'm not angry. I just need to concentrate." This worked perfectly for the remainder of my tenure.

o   o   o

One experience I had was with a former manager and having the "I know" attitude. This manager had a very strong Type A personality, and every task had to be completed a certain way, regardless of new ideas and feedback from employees within that department. What worked in one company doesn't always work the same in another. I know that many other employees brought this blind spot to the person's attention.

o   o   o

My inability to delegate and control things too closely [is a blind spot]. I have worked hard to empower those around me. I was overwhelmed when first becoming a manager, and someone more senior than me coached me on how to share the workload among my team and trust them to do a good job. I started to see those around me flourish.

o   o   o

A project manager who wanted to become a senior project manager didn't understand why he wasn't getting the support from the team. It required a candid conversation with specific examples for him to realize why he wasn't getting everyone's support. He was blind about what was important to everyone else and about how self-defeating his behaviors were.

He became aware of it from a conversation I had with him with specific examples. His blind spot had been holding him back for his entire career, preventing him from achieving his goals.

○   ○   ○

During my previous employment I was recruited for a position to increase the physical and cyber security of [an organization]. During face-to-face meetings, I was very clear that I would need resources and gave a general idea of what I thought those needs would be based on experience without an exact understanding of their internal capability.

Once I started the position I quickly tried to understand operations. However, I was given no direction, so I took it upon myself to start evaluating capabilities and needs. My director seemed annoyed that I was taking the initiative...he blocked most all of my suggestions until I decided to go around him and submit a proposal to the executive director. From that point, the executive director told me to not let anyone know we were working together on changes, even though he was three rungs up in my chain of command.

This secrecy made weekly production meetings very strange for me. I believe that my director had a large blind spot overestimating his ability to understand a topic he had no formal training or experience in. He also was not aware how to communicate with others. I think he thought he was sociable, but when matters arose, he resorted to threats. I do not think he ever realized his challenges. The relationship between me and my director resulted in my leaving [the organization] after 16 years of service.

Build Your Personal Brand

As you evaluate your progress with overcoming blind spots, repeat the process we've outlined often, and continually learn from others' mistakes, you will build your personal brand. Our personal brand is what people think of when they think of us. The people who know us best base their conclusions on things like how we spend our time, what we're passionate about, what we celebrate, what we won't tolerate, and how we respond to various situations. Those we rarely engage with determine our personal brand based on how we portray ourselves through such things as our attire, language, experiences, social media posts, etc.

We all have a personal brand we want to communicate to others…but is what we are saying what we desire? Have you stopped to think about how you want to be perceived? When my (Brian) children were young and uninhibited, I asked them, "What do I really care about?" and the answers were very insightful for me as a father. Another thing I have done on occasion is ask on social media, "What do you perceive that I really care about?" This gives me an insight into my personal brand. At other times, I've asked similar questions: "How would you describe me in five words?" or "What do you see I am really passionate about?" Most of the time I get responses like faith, family, leadership, communication, and community service. Some would add things like O.U. (University of Oklahoma) football and cool socks! Knowing how we're perceived can help us to be motivated to make changes that are important for our career, relationships, and effectiveness.

The following is a set of questions and insights for you to work through as you identify and work on blind spots throughout your life. Return to these questions and your answers often—you may even see how your responses evolve over time.

Defining Your Personal Brand

1. Define branding in six sentences or less.
2. What do you desire your personal professional brand to be? We're not discounting how your personal brand is reflected at home, but we want your personal branding to focus on the professional side.
3. Of those who know you professionally, what percent do you believe think of you in the way that you describe in question #2? Why is that?
4. How do most of your professional contacts think of you? (What brand do they see?) Be specific.
5. Where is the gap? What is the difference between the way you want to be perceived and the way you are perceived?
6. What have you done in the last 10 years to contribute to a perception that is different than what you want your personal brand to be? Be as exhaustive as possible.
7. Pause. Take 24 hours to let these insights simmer.
8. In light of your responses to items 1–7, what needs to happen in order to move closer to your ideal personal brand? What do you need to start doing? Stop doing? Continue doing?
9. Is there anyone that you need to go to and apologize and seek forgiveness from?
10. What weekly activities could you schedule in the next 90 days that would accomplish this personal professional brand makeover?

Putting in the Work

It had been a long day of leading a training on public speaking and presentation skills for a company, and now we were making our way home on a seven-hour journey. A colleague was driving and I (Brian) was enjoying the rare opportunity to sit back and relax in the passenger seat. In the distance, I saw emergency lights flashing on top of a vehicle in the opposite lane. I soon realized that it was a large wrecker parked on the side of the road, the kind that was capable of pulling semi-trucks. But what I saw next was completely unexpected and an image I'll never forget. A 300–350 pound man was hanging out of the driver's door, upside down, waving frantically at everyone who was going by!

Dozens of cars passed him without so much as flashing their brakes, seemingly oblivious or unwilling to address the dangerous predicament. Later as I tried to justify their complacency, I assumed that some of the drivers didn't notice because they were watching other spots on the road or were preoccupied with the strains and stresses of life. But a multi-ton vehicle with flashing lights and a man hanging upside down and waving should have certainly drawn the attention of somebody other than us!

As we made a U-turn, a state trooper pulled behind us and we both approached the wrecker. Together, we silently evaluated the situation, determined the issue, and began to remedy the problem.

So, you're probably wondering what the issue was. The driver had had a stroke as he was driving down the highway. He was finally able to pull the vehicle to the side of the road. As he attempted to exit the vehicle and get help, his foot had gotten caught on wires under the dashboard. And he had dropped his phone. I'll never know how long he had been struggling there or what would have happened if we or the trooper hadn't stopped. But I'm glad we did.

What about you? Once you've identified a problem, will you stop your current path, make a U-turn, and deal with the issue? Or will you just look the other way and act as if everything is normal?

You know the issues that are stalling your potential, but now you also know strategies for how to tackle them. You've hopefully discovered both the items that are tripping you up and some new strengths alike. If you put in the work, get ready to be more successful in your career and experience greater connectivity with those around you. As you grow, your confidence will increase, and you'll be open to taking on challenges that previously seemed out of your reach. We've seen it time and again where people—even whole organizations—addressed issues that had previously been swept under the rug and then they started hitting their goals, increasing their revenue, and having a broader reach of influence.

We have found and continue to find the blind spots in our own lives as well. Yes, we wrote the book for you, but we've also experienced these benefits. We can all discover new strengths, find new talents, improve relationships, change perceptions, and alter our behavior for the better. In the words of hockey legend Wayne Gretzky, "You miss 100% of the shots you don't take." We challenge you as a lifelong learner to continuously seek out and address the blind spots in your life. The only thing you will regret is not trying.

○   ○   ○

Personal Reflection

- Complete the first two questions regarding Defining Your Personal Brand. Then review your answers.

    1. Define branding in six sentences or less.

    2. What do you desire your personal brand to be?

- What do you think is the number one issue threatening your ability to make the changes regarding your blind spot permanent? Be specific.

Group Discussion

- What do you desire your personal brand to be?

- Why do you want that brand?

- How has your brand changed over time?

- Ask the group for feedback on how well you are developing this brand so far.

APPENDIX

APPENDIX A

Personal Feedback Worksheet

P ersonal feedback is essential to discovering blind spots. Choose three people who would be honest with you about your personality and behavior. Ask them the General and/or Specific questions below. To use the more specific set of questions, you and your feedback partners will agree to focus on a designated recent event or situation at work for a reference point. What insights did you discover about yourself?

Personal Feedback Form–General

Use this to find out more about your behavior and personality

- How am I perceived by most people?

- What do you consider to be my top three greatest strengths?

- What good and bad patterns have you observed about me?

- What areas would you like to see me improve?

- What areas need improvement that you think I'm unaware of?

Personal Feedback Form–Specific

Focus on a specific situation at work or a certain event in your personal life

- What did I do well?

- What areas could I improve?

- What did you notice about the way I carried myself?

- Where did I miss the mark on execution?

- Was I clear in my communication? Why or why not?

- How could I have been more prepared?

APPENDIX B

Blind Spot Action Plan

Walk through the following set of questions for each blind spot that you are considering working on. Write your answers in a journal and review them often.

Blind Spot #1:_____

- Why is the blind spot worth dealing with?

- What are the pros of taking action and the cons of not taking action?

- Now list as many options as possible for potential actions you could take to deal with your blind spot.
    1.
    2.
    3.

- Who could you enlist to help you?

- What resources should you utilize?

- How will you know if you're successful?

APPENDIX C

Common Blind Spots and Suggested Actions

U sing the information you've gleaned in this book, complete some or all of the list of Suggested Actions to address common blind spot areas.

Common Blind Spot	Suggested Actions
Acting entitled	In each situation, find a way to help someone else.
Laziness	Hold yourself accountable to making good use of your time by scheduling your day.
Failure to contribute	
No accountability/Passing the buck/Lack of ownership or personal responsibility	
Talking too much	
Talking too little	
Negative facial expressions	

Negative self-storytelling	
Harshness	
Too soft (doormat mentality)	
Black-and-white attitude/ judgmental	
Wishy-washy	
Overly pessimistic	
Overly optimistic	
Too trusting	
Competitive	
Working too fast	
Working too slowly	

Failure to listen	
Critical/picky	
Materialistic	
Offensive sense of humor	
Short fuse	
Slobby appearance, messiness	
Lack of tact	
Anal retentive	
Showy (name dropping, using big words)	
Focusing on too much detail	
Keeping up with the Joneses	

Too frugal/cheap	
Bad language and word choice	
Inappropriate clothing choices	
Reputation	
Flaky/undependable	
Lack of personal growth/ improvement	
Believing/buying into stereotypes	
"This is the way we have always done it" mentality	
Lack of leadership	
Interrupting others	

ACKNOWLEDGMENTS

We could not begin to thank all of the people who have contributed to this book in one way or another.

However, we are both grateful to our spouses and children who gave us great feedback...and sometimes unknowingly provided content.

Ann Terese, Jeremy, Katie, and Heidi Brandt have been hearing about blind spots and the ideas for this book for nearly a dozen years. Thanks for the love and support along the way!

Andy, Caden, Ryder, and Willow Kutach have provided a fun and entertaining home to recharge. Thanks for always being willing to exchange ideas, laugh at ourselves, and love each other!

We're also grateful to our parents, siblings, mentors, colleagues, clients, and friends who have both shared ideas and encouraged us.

ABOUT CORE INSIGHTS

Core Insights has consistently developed clients' personnel and expanded their vision while becoming a trusted partner, not a vendor of services. Bringing many years of experience and education to the issues companies face, we take companies to new heights.

Developing people is our greatest strength. With a deep understanding of adult education and effective training, and a wide breadth of experience with countless industries, we utilize proven methods to help employees have "aha moments" to gain new soft skills.

Whether you're in healthcare, banking and finance, manufacturing, technology, non-profit, or the myriad of other industries we serve, our expertise in training and strategic planning help expand the capacity of your team and the direction of your organization.

Visit us at **www.CoreInsightsLeadership.com**.

ENDNOTES

1. Heather Buchman, "Joplin Tragedy Teaches Lessons on Saving Lives," https://www.accuweather.com/en/weather-news/severe-weather-warnings-someth/55287, September, 2011. Accessed January 2018.

2. The term Emotional Intelligence did not surface until Wayne Payne's 1985 doctoral dissertation entitled "A study of emotion: developing emotional intelligence; self-integration; relating to fear, pain and desire (theory, structure of reality, problem-solving, contraction/expansion, tuning in/coming out/letting go"). But the concept has been researched for almost a century. Researchers including Edward Thorndike, David Wechsler, Abraham Maslow, and Howard Gardner identified a variety of related concepts, including social intelligence, emotional strength, and multiple intelligences.

3. Peter Salovey and John Mayer published their landmark article "Emotional Intelligence" in the journal *Imagination, Cognition, and Personality* (1990). Daniel Goleman, author of *Emotional Intelligence: Why It Can Matter More Than IQ* (1995), is also a great source on this topic.

4. Tiger Woods' Apology: Full Transcript, CNN, http://edition.cnn.com/2010/US/02/19/tiger.woods.transcript/index.html. Accessed January 2019.